THEOLOGY
OF PRAYER

THEOLOGY
OF PRAYER

Rev. John A. Hardon, S.J.

ST. PAUL EDITIONS

IMPRIMI POTEST:
    Richard T. Clearly, S.J.
    Provincial

NIHIL OBSTAT:
    Richard V. Lawlor, S.J.
    Censor Deputatus

IMPRIMATUR:
    + Humberto Cardinal Medeiros
    Archbishop of Boston

Library of Congress Cataloging in Publication Data

Hardon, John A
    The theology of prayer.

    1. Prayer.   I.   Title.
BV210.2.H364   248'.3   79-1400

Photo credits:
R. Dolan, 10
Pilgrim Productions Rockland, Ma., 32, 80, 162

Printed in the U.S.A. by the Daughters of St. Paul
50 St. Paul's Ave., Boston, Ma: 02130

The Daughters of St. Paul are an international
congregation of religious women serving the Church
with the communications media.

CONTENTS

The Meaning of Prayer

Some explanation may be necessary for going into such an obvious subject as, the meaning of prayer. Why not start with something more practical, like, how to pray, or how to improve our prayer, and not begin with what must seem like needless concern with words, here, the meaning of prayer. But I do not think it is wasted effort to talk about what so many people are not doing, or not doing as well as they could. On all sides we hear it said that the basic problem in the world today is the fact that people are not praying, or not praying enough, and this is true. But it is not enough to say that we should pray and should encourage others to do the same. We had better also know what prayer really means. Otherwise, as has happened to so many, we and they, may, I do not say give up prayer, but not profit as much as we should for what is by all odds the most profitable enterprise in which any person can engage. There is nothing more profitable in which any human being can engage than to pray.

We begin therefore by describing prayer in as simple a language as we, that is, I can. Prayer is conversation with the invisible world of God, the angels and the saints. We shall take each one of these terms in sequence, and first talk about prayer as *conversation.*

What is conversation, any conversation with anyone? Or from another viewpoint, what do we do when we engage someone in conversation? We do several things.

First. We begin to converse with somebody when we become *aware* of that person. Awareness, then, is the first condition for conversation. Suppose I am just talking out loud to myself without realizing that I am being overheard. Is that conversation? Well, no. Why not? Because I was not aware of the other person's presence. If I was doing anything I was in conversation with myself. In fact, I think most people spend most of their waking hours in self-conversation, which is called, to give it a kind term, soliloquy. Whereas, true conversation is always a colloquy. It is not only awareness, but awareness of someone else's presence besides my own. And so many people go through life, I'm afraid, only dimly aware of anyone else's presence, except their own. That is why self-centered people, even when they are apparently in conversation out loud with someone else are most often really talking to themselves. Ever watch it? It is a spectacle.

Real conversation begins when I become aware of an*other*, with stress on the *other*, and not only of myself.

Second. Besides being aware of someone, and it has to be someone else, conversation means that I wish to share with that other person something of what I have. I wish to give of myself, of what is inside of me, or a part of me to that other person. There are thoughts on my mind that I want the other person to have also. There are sentiments in my heart, desires in my will and feelings in my soul, that I do not wish to possess alone. So I enter into conversation in order to share. So true is this, that logically and psychologically I should not begin a conversation, unless I have something that I wish to give someone else, which presumably that person does not yet have. That is why the highest act of charity among human beings is conversation, provided it is genuine and not spurious conversation.

Third. There is still more to conversation, as the very word implies. When I begin to converse, I literally turn towards the one with whom I wish to speak. The movement of my body facing that person is only the external symbol of what I should be doing inside of me. I am turning my spirit towards the one with whom I wish to talk. But as we know, it is quite possible to be physically facing someone without really conversing. There is no conversation worthy of the name, unless I have thus inwardly turned aside from self and directed myself to another. We seldom reflect on the fact that the words convert, conversion and conversation, all have the same fundamental meaning of re-direction, a turning away from one thing, in this case self, and toward something else, in this case another person. True, sincere, deep, genuine, total conversation is more rare than we think. So often I believe we use other people, as we say, as sounding boards—to listen to our own voice. They are just convenient to help us in what is still a continuous soliloquy. All real conversation, therefore, has this element of self-denial, or from another viewpoint, self-sacrifice, where I turn from preoccupation with my own thoughts and desires and direct them towards someone else.

Fourth. What is my purpose when I hold a conversation? My purpose is, or should be to communicate. My intention is to bridge the gap that separates me from another person to unite myself with that other person, in a word, to communicate by transferring something of what is me to become part of what is he or she. We become united mainly by what we share of our own spirit with another person. Our Savior expressed for all time the deep meaning of conversation as communication when He told the apostles how they were no longer strangers to Him but His friends (cf. Jn. 15:15). Why? Because "I have shared with you what is in me. I've told you what, before I spoke, was only on my mind. Now it's also on your minds. We have become united because part of me is now part of you. You and I are united because I have communicated to you what before I spoke to you was only mine." And then to emphasize the gravity of what He was doing He said it was the Father who first in conversation with the Son had shared the plenitude of the divine nature, so that the Son in turn might share of that fullness with others who would mainly become His children because they would now receive what before belonged only to the Trinity. "You belong to me," still Christ in paraphrase, "and I belong to you because we now have in common the secrets that were hidden with God from all eternity." We might, with reverence, re-describe the Trinity as the eternal, infinite conversation among the Three Persons who constitute the Deity.

We are still on the subject of conversation, if you please, and we're not finished yet.

Fifth and finally. Every conversation in some way or other employs a response from the one to whom I am speaking. Conversation is not merely talking to someone; it is talking with someone. Unless that person also says something to me I may be giving a speech or making an announcement, but I am hardly conversing. The way that person responds to me is immaterial. It may be just a smile, or depending on what I said, a frown. It may be only an occasional word or two; it may be only a yes with different inflections. You know, of course, there are at least fifty ways of saying yes, *yes*, yes. No matter what I say to that person, it must evoke something that he says to me or we are not, in the deepest sense of the word, in conversation. It takes two, at least two to converse, even when one may do most of the talking, and the other, or others, do most of the listening. I should add, just for the record, that when I speak publicly, besides looking at the script I mainly watch the eyes and faces of my audience. I want to make sure that we are in conversation.

So much for the first level of our reflection.

We said that prayer was first of all and fundamentally conversation. But this is no ordinary conversation; it is conversation with the invisible world. As conversation, prayer does not essentially differ from all other forms of colloquial discourse. But prayer is no ordinary conversation. It is conversation with the invisible world whose existence we can partially reason to, and then only quite dimly, but whose reality and grandeur we can fully know only by faith. Why call this world invisible? Because it is not seen with the eyes of the body, but is known only with the eyes of the mind. It is not only not visible to the eyes of the body, but also not audible with bodily ears, or tangible with bodily hands or palatable with bodily lips or perceptible with any of the bodily senses. And sadly, how tragically, some people suppose that because it is not sensibly perceptible therefore it is not real. It is a world of faith that really exists and as St. Paul tells us is actually more real than the mountains, rivers and seas and more important than even the most important people we could ever meet on earth who might give us—if they would—a few minutes' private audience or personal interview and we would treasure the memory of those moments for the rest of our days.

Prayer depends on the liveliness of our faith. Without faith there is no prayer. Either I believe that there is more to reality that the sun, moon and stars, and more than the people I meet on the streets or in the privacy of my home, or I shall not pray. I shall limit my conversation to the visible world and that is not prayer. Those who believe, pray; those who do not believe, do not pray. Those who believe much, pray much; those who believe little, pray little. Those who believe deeply, pray deeply; those who believe weakly, pray weakly. We pray as we believe, neither more nor less.

Faith is the condition for prayer. It is also the measure and the norm of the quality and quantity of our prayer. Faith tells us that the so-called invisible world in which we believe is greater by all standards than the visible world of space and time. It is more numerous, more powerful, more experienced, more beautiful, and much more holy, thank God, than the present world in which we live. It is a world that we sometimes mistakenly call the next world. It is not next at all, as though it still had to come into being whereas it already exists. Who says it's the next world? It is a world that is deeply conscious of our existence, even when we are not conscious of its existence, and is very interested in our welfare. It is a world that is more easily accessible actually than the world that surrounds us. It is therefore the world that is readily available for our conversation if only we have the faith and the vision to see. None of us wants to talk to no one.

GOD

We begin then by asking ourselves who belongs to this invisible world. The first one who is more than a part of this invisible world, with whom we are privileged to communicate is God. He is the supreme Spirit, who alone exists of Himself, and is infinite in all His perfections. He is utterly distinct in reality and essence from all other things that exist or can be conceived; all of which, if they exist, get their existence from Him. God is eternal, without beginning, end or succession; all-knowing even of man's most secret thoughts. He knows them before we tell Him. He is immeasurable, being at once in heaven and on earth. He is in all places that are or that can be. He is just in rendering to everyone according to his due in this world or hereafter. Nor is that all. The God of faith is not a solitary Deity but the eternal society of Father, Son and Spirit. Each truly and fully God, and therefore truly distinct, yet all together being but one divine nature, so that there is only one God. What communication has been going on among the three divine Persons from endless ages before the world began! What a conversation they have been having long before any creature existed, or any human being even had a thought. You might again with reverence say that when we pray to God we are breaking in on the conversation among the Persons in the Trinity.

THE ANGELS

If God is the first and primary Being of the invisible world, with whom we are called upon to speak, the angels are the second great beings with whom we are to communicate in prayer. Who are the angels? They are the heavenly spirits created by God before He made the visible world and the human race. Not a few Fathers of the Church say seriously: "In God's original plan of creation there was only to have been this invisible created world. But part of that created world sinned, so to replace—must have been a lot of places—to fill heaven with those who would honor Him for eternity He then decided to create mankind."

The angels are pure spirits who have no bodies like our own but they are persons no less than we. They are intelligent beings whom God brought into being to praise, love and serve Him no less than us. They are the angels who proved their loyalty to God and are now in heaven with God, never to be separated from Him. Their role in God's plan for the universe, and how this bears emphasis, is to serve our needs. They are literally the guardians of the human race. And it is part of our faith that each one of us has his or her own guardian spirit. Guardian angels are consequently part of God's supernatural providence, which as we know works through creatures from the higher to the lower—needless to say we are the lower. Within the realm of created beings the angels are more like God because they are pure creatures having no body, but they are also like us because we too have a mind and a will, so we can talk to the angels. The angels are providential intermediaries between God, whose vision they already enjoy, and mankind, whom they are entrusted to lead to the vision not yet attained. We therefore have not only the privilege but the duty to talk with the angels in easy, intimate and frequent conversation.

We read in the lives of the saints how friendly some of them were in their prayerful communication with the angels. Why not? Each one of us has a constant, daily companion at our side, whose responsibility is not only to guard us from evil, but to guide us in the ways of God. He is often talking to us if only we are ready to hear. And a large part of our prayer with the angels, especially our own guardian spirit, should be humbly listening to what he has to say.

THE SAINTS

There is one more level of the invisible world of prayer with which we are to converse beyond God and the angels, and that is the universe of the saints. By the saints we here mean first and mainly those men and women whom the Church has raised to the honors of the altar and has infallibly declared to be with God in glory. One of the less well-known passages of the Second Vatican Council occurs in the Constitution on the Church where we are urged to be more responsive to the invisible world of the saints on high. We are told, "It is not merely by the title of example that we cherish the memory of those in heaven. We seek rather that by this devotion to the exercise of fraternal charity the union of the whole Church in the Spirit may be strengthened. Exactly as Christian communion between people on their earthly pilgrimage brings us closer to Christ, so our communion with the saints joins us to Christ from whom as from its fountain and head issues all grace and the very life of the people of God."

The saints behold the face of God. By speaking with them and listening to them we learn much about this God whom they now know as we hope one day to understand. And they can help us as only those who have reached their destiny can assist those — that is us — who are still in such desperate need.

I have a short epilogue. I would like to end these reflections where we began, by asking ourselves and answering our own question, "What is the meaning of prayer?" Prayer is the sublime conversation we are mysteriously able to hold with the invisible world of God and of God's angels and saints. It is sublime because that is what we are preparing for during our stay on earth. Prayer is the one activity that will not be interrupted by death, but will continue in heaven, never to end. Of course prayer on earth requires effort, but that is as it should be, since all other labor in this life has only as much value and as much meaning, and is only as pleasing to God as it is enveloped by prayer. Those who pray now will pray in eternity, which is another name for heaven. No one else will get there. Prayer is the indispensable and infallible means of reaching our destiny.

Prayer of Admiration and Praise

If we were to ask the average Catholic what he means by prayer, I think he would say something like this: "Prayer is asking God for what you need." The answer is correct, of course, but not fully adequate. No doubt many people, maybe most people, most of the time when they pray are asking God for some favor, whether something they want, or to be protected from something they don't want. They are sick and in pain, and so they pray for health. They face a difficult situation and so they pray for light and strength to cope with the problem. They are confused and bewildered so they ask God to give them some guidance. They are afraid of what awaits them in the future and so they pray for courage.

All of this is true, and is as it should be. In fact, one reason that God sends us trials and difficulties is to keep us humbly dependent on His help. He knows, how well He knows, that if everything always went well we would become proud and independent and would likely not pray. And the pages of the Gospel are filled with episodes in which people in trouble asked the Savior for help. It seems that is all they were doing. "Lord, that I may see." "Lord, if you wish you can make me whole." "If I but touch the hem of his garment I shall get well." "Jesus, Son of David, have pity on me."

But is that all there is to prayer, or more exactly, is this the highest form of prayer in which we can engage, the prayer in which we tell God, "Lord, come to my assistance; make haste to help me"?

ADORATION

The answer to our question is no. The most sublime prayer we can offer to God is not the prayer of petition. It is not even the prayer of gratitude. It is the prayer of adoration. This prayer of adoration is implicit in every other prayer that we make and without this no one would ever really pray at all. The only reason we ask God to help us is because we first acknowledge who He is. The only reason we ever thank God for anything is because, implicit in our gratitude, is already adoration.

What do we do when we adore God? When we adore God we recognize who He is, and tell Him we are pleased. That second part is not an afterthought. You know we can tell people who or what we think they are, but besides saying that, we must also be pleased. I believe that much more attention should be given to the prayer of adoration than we are naturally inclined to give. I say this especially because today's world is so preoccupied with self, and with man's own achievements, so interested in what human genius has discovered or human ingenuity has made. Man is preoccupied with man.

In my opinion the capital sin of the present age is self-idolatry. Men and women are so lost in their personal or collective accomplishments that they are literally, though we don't use the words, they are literally adoring themselves. The malady then is more serious than just not asking God for His assistance. It is the deeper vice of ignoring the majesty of God and worshipping instead the pathetically finite misery of man. How otherwise explain what otherwise defies explanation — human beings standing in judgment on the most sacred laws of the Almighty. He tells them to honor father and mother and all legitimate superiors in society. They tell Him that *they* determine who has authority, how and even what authority means, and not He. He tells them not to commit adultery or fornication, or homosexuality. They tell Him to mind His own divine business. They are not children any more, as were the simple believers of a former age, to be told how to enjoy their own bodies. He tells them not to shed innocent human blood. They tell Him that they are masters of life and death, and not He. It is not for Him but for them to decide who shall live before birth or after birth, and for how long.

In one of my conversations recently with Mother Teresa on this subject, she told me she was convinced the real evil behind the evil of abortion is not mere selfishness, it is not merely that people are so preoccupied with their own interests as not to want children to stand between themselves and the pleasures they can enjoy. Behind the mania of abortion, she's convinced, certainly in the leaders of society, is a defiance of God. I agree. If we were to speculate how man in his maddest treachery could defy the Almighty from the depths of his being would it not be precisely in the act of procreation? Here God tells man, "I am Master of life and death," and man's evil genius has invented a way to say no to the Creator by denying God's right over human existence. If ever, surely today, God wants adorers in spirit and in truth to make up for the blasphemers in untruth. He wants men, women and children to adore Him. When I have occasion I recommend to mothers and fathers that they cannot begin too early with the children to teach them to acknowledge God as God in all the accents of human language. Why? In order to make up for the massive denial of adoration by so many who are seduced by one another's achievement and become drunk with their own self-conceit. Adoration is the primary duty of man as creature. God demands man's adoration as the fundamental law of human existence.

ADMIRATION

If we were to look more closely at what this prayer of divine adoration means we would find that it means the admiration of God. What a strange expression, "admiring God"! Yet that is what adoring God first means. It means that the human mind on beholding God's greatness is lost in wonder at who He is. When we admire someone we marvel with satisfaction at who he is or what he has or how he could have done what he did. All admiration is wonderment at what seems to be a contradiction or beyond normal explanation. If this is true of any creature, even the most marvelous, what shall we say about God? Everything about Him is a paradox because everything in Him is a mystery that no one but God can fully understand. The greatest wonder of wonders is God, and He wants us to tell Him how wonderful He is. He is at once the most merciful, and yet the most just. Where do you find, I don't say perfect, but even a balanced combination of these two qualities in human beings? He is utterly hidden and yet totally present. He is most beautiful and yet the most strong. He Himself undergoes no change but He changes all things. God is never new. Strange! He's never old but making everything else new. God is always active. Philosophers define Him as pure act, yet He is perfectly at rest. He is gathering and inviting all things to Himself yet He needs nothing and no one. He sustains and fulfills; He protects and creates; He nourishes and makes perfect everything. He is always demanding and yet lacking nothing. You would think He needed everything; He needs nothing, but all creatures need Him. Is it any wonder that the mystics have exhausted the words of created wisdom in trying to describe the marvelous Being who is God?

Among the prayers of admiration in the Church's treasury, the one of St. Augustine speaks, I think, for the rest of us who lack the genius of St. Monica's son saying to God, "How wonderful You are."

I quote Augustine:

"You love without subjection to passion.
You are jealous but not with fear.
You can know repentance but not sorrow,
  be angry and unperturbed by anger.
You can change the things You have made
  but Your mind remains changeless.
You find and receive back what You never
  lost;
    are never in need but rejoice over Your
    gains;
    are not greedy but demand interest
    manifold.
Men pay You more than they have to in
  order to win from You in return,
yet who has anything which is not already
  Yours?
You owe nothing, yet pay as if You were
  in debt to Your creatures.
Forgive what is owed to You, yet without
  losing thereby.
And with all this what have I said,
  My God and my life and my sacred
  delight.
What can anyone say when he speaks
  to You?
Yet woe to them who are silent about You.
When even those who say most are but
  dumb."

Adoring God, however, is not only admiring
Him, although admiration is the principal
form of adoration. When we admire God, I
think we have to get used to the vocabulary
"admiring God." When we admire Him we
look as it were directly into His face and tell
Him how marvelous He is, and how pleased we
are that He is God. He loves such prayer of
admiration, and in fact, He created rational

creatures both angels and men in the final analysis in order to receive their homage — this kind of homage of adoration shown in admiration which they freely give Him as their God.

If we have any doubt of how pleased God must be when we tell Him how wonderful He is, let's just remember the times, I hope many times, that people have told us, "How wonderful you are!" Remember? We were thrilled. As wives tell me, there are no words they more want to hear from their husbands than for the husbands to look at them and say, "You are wonderful."

Adoration, however, has another form of expression and this is praise. Praise builds on admiration, and in this case looks upon God indeed, but adores Him not so much in Himself as in the creatures He has made. The words of revelation are filled with passages of praise for the wonderful creatures that, except for God, would not exist, and except for their existence God would not be praised.

As we reread the Gospels and see how often people marveled at what Christ did — and we are told by the evangelists they praised God — it is remarkable how often Christ had to go beyond the wonders of nature to work miracles which, by the way, are nothing else than God's dramatic way of calling attention to His presence on earth in order to evoke admiration and to solicit man's praise.

The word miracle simply means something marvelous. In German — I like the expression — a miracle is *wunder,* wonder. And God would actually, we can humanly say, have spared Himself the trouble of working extra wonders, which are marvelous and therefore evoke admiration and praise, except that human beings are so blind to the wonders already in creation that He works supplementary wonders that we call wonderful. Why? Not because God is any more godly in working a miracle, but because they happen so seldom that at long last we marvel and call it a miracle. If we look closely at the Church's liturgy we find there no less than in the Gospels numerous invitations to adoring God by praising Him. Once again we turn to the mystics to make their sentiments our own. This time we find in St. Francis of Assisi's Canticle of the Sun one of the purest professions of praise of the Godhead in Christian hagiography. Even those who are not Christians admire its sentiments and all of us can make them our own.

"O most High, Almighty, good Lord,
to you belong praise, glory, honor and all
blessing.
Praised be my Lord God with all His
creatures,
and especially our Brother the Sun
who brings us the day and brings us the
night.
Fair is he and shines with a very great
splendor.
O Lord, he signifies you to us.
Praised be my Lord for our Sister the
Moon
and for the stars which he has set clear and
lovely in heaven.
Praised be my Lord for our Brother the
Wind
and for the air and clouds, calms and all
weather
by which you uphold life in all creatures.

Praised be my Lord for our Sister Water who
is very serviceable to us,
and humble and precious and very clean.
Praised be my Lord for our Brother Fire
through which you give us light in the
darkness.
He is bright and pleasant and very mighty
and strong.
Praised be my Lord for our Mother the Earth
which sustains us and keeps us,
and brings forth grass and diverse fruits
and flowers of many kinds.
Praise and bless the Lord and give thanks
to Him
and serve Him with great humility. Amen."

As one who has been brought up by a
Franciscan tertiary mother, and who long
before I discovered Ignatius knew Francis,
I can assure you that many people misunder-
stand the mysticism of Francis. Or they fail to
realize, and this is the worst tragedy, that in
praising all the varied creatures and in sensing
such close intimacy with them what Francis
was doing was adoring God. He saw as only
mystics can see in every creature, even the
lowliest, the majesty of God. He could hardly
bring himself to kill a fly. What he saw in
creatures is what the Church, in giving us men
like him for imitation, wants us to learn. It is
the fact that behind every creature is the creative
power of God; that except for His will and His
love no creature would exist; that every creature
is a divine invitation to praise the Creator.
Praising God in practice means using God's
creatures indeed but never stopping with them
but seeing beyond them and behind them and
beneath them not only God's original act of

creation but His constant, sustaining divine power which I praise whenever I use even the least of the things that God made.

There are more vistas to prayer—that is, the prayer of adoration—than the two we have just seen, of admiration and praise. But no other form of prayer is higher or deeper than this. None is higher because it is this kind of prayer that the angels have been saying, though we, for want of a better word, say "have been singing" since the dawn of their creation, and that all intelligent creation is destined to be praying into all the reaches of eternity.

No form of prayer is deeper because when we adore God we are in contact with infinity and although still creatures are talking with the Almighty who was, and who is and ever will be. We are, how prosaic the word sounds, we are in conversation with God.

Prayer and the Grace of God

The popular understanding of prayer as asking for God's help is correct. Most of the prayers in the Scriptures are petitions. Most of the prayers of the liturgy are the same. And even the acts of adoration or love are always implicit petitions for divine assistance. And Christ tells us to ask, to seek, to knock—clearly all petitions. So that we ask, "why?" Why do we need to ask for God's help? The reason is the obvious one: because we *need* that help. However, since we are talking about God and God is not obvious, this cannot be all that obvious as may seem.

We need God's help because we are creatures, because we have a fallen human nature, and because we are being constantly beseiged by the evil spirit. The first reason then that we must pray for help is because we are creatures whom God has raised to an above-creaturely destiny. Sometimes I think we should more often use the expression "supercreaturely" or "supercreated" instead of the by now prosaic "supernatural." We have been destined for heaven, but heaven is not natural to anyone. Anyone? That's right! Except whom? God! Consequently, having been destined for heaven—and what could be clearer—we are not there yet, we cannot get there by merely human or created means. We need what we call—because some term had to be coined and St. Paul coined it—we need grace which may be described as what we need but do not of ourselves possess in order to reach the heavenly beatitude for which we were made. What we have is nature; where we are going is heaven; what we need is grace.

But, then comes an embarrassing question: Do we mean to say that, although God destined us for heaven, He did not give us the means for getting there? Well, yes and no. He will give us the means, but we do not have those means unless we ask for them. Asking for the means to reach heaven is another word for prayer. We, therefore, affirm that in God's ordinary providence we shall not receive what we need, namely grace, unless we beg for what we need. This is a hard saying, but it is profoundly true. Of ourselves, not only as individuals, but even working together with other human beings, neither I can reach heaven nor can we reach heaven. I and we need divine grace. One of the most pathetic features of modern society, speaking of society, is the foolish idea put into wide practice that as individuals we cannot make it, but as members of society just cooperating with other people we can make it. Make what? Well, make whatever the society has been established to do!

We need divine light and divine strength beyond our natural light and strength to save ourselves as social beings and barring a miracle we cannot obtain this light or this strength without prayer—whether for us for what we need personally or for ourselves for what we need corporately and socially. The main reason why human society is in such chaos is that human society has not been invoking divine aid.

This past Sunday I spoke in the beautiful St. John the Baptist Church in Manhattan, the Provincial and American headquarters of the Fathers of the Blessed Sacrament. I spoke appropriately on the day of the canonization of St. John Neumann on the Eucharist and Sanctity. After the conference to a crowded church we had a procession. I carried the Blessed Sacrament. More than once I told our Lord: "You are heavy." We walked and we walked—it must have been a mile—through all the aisles of the church. That procession was the social prayer of that congregation. It was the people praying and singing as they walked. And one of the pities, the director of the peoples' Eucharistic League who sponsored the affair, told me: "We are not allowed to process with the Blessed Sacrament outside." Whatever we can do to restore processions in these not-so-Christian United States will be blessed by God because we need to invoke His grace not only as individuals but as societies. There are a thousand ways of doing so. Processions—the last thing I thought I would say—are one way of corporately asking for divine grace.

We need prayer, therefore, as individuals, prayer as groups, to remain in God's friendship. Without prayer we will lose the divine life we possess, and more obviously, we shall not grow in the life we already have. In other words, no prayer, no salvation. This is the basic reason why we are seeing such tragedies among once apparently strong believers. For being a believer is no guarantee of remaining one. They did not pray, or pray enough, or pray with sufficient constancy or perseverance, so the inevitable happened. They lacked the humility to admit their impotency to keep God's commandments by themselves. In a word, they lacked the grace they needed, and they lacked it because they failed to pray. And we dare not say that God owes us the grace — that is a contradiction in terms. Grace is precisely that which God does not owe us. That is why we correctly speak of begging.

One who begs asks for that to which he has no right. That is grace! We are beggars by the definition of our supernatural destiny. That is the first reason: we are creatures and we are made to possess the infinite God. That God will not be possessed except by those who when they die are in the grace of God. They will get that grace and retain it only if they pray.

The second reason why we need to pray — because we have passions. From another viewpoint we must pray because we have a fallen human nature and the correct word is not "falling," but "fallen." Sure we have been justified, sure. Please God, we have been restored to God's friendship, but that does not change our nature from having been and being a fallen nature.

As a consequence of our fallen state we have all sorts of unruly desires and fears that we call our passions. We need divine help to cope with these urges which differ with different people. You might almost say what distinguishes us as persons is that each one of us has his or her own special unique passions. What turns one person on, turns another person off. But, although they differ so much in their variety, they are all fundamentally the same as passions.

Except for Christ and His Blessed Mother who we are certain were exempt from the stain of original sin and therefore had no concupiscences, the rest of us must either pray constantly for the grace to overcome our concupiscence or we shall give in to our irrational drives. Anger and pride and lust, covetousness and envy and sloth and gluttony are not only the names of the seven capital sins, they are the names of the seven capital drives. They are the seven deadly enemies of our soul synthesized by the Apostle in that one simple word, "our flesh." And these drives, be it said, are not only in the flesh, though they go by the generic name of "the flesh," because they are in our fallen human natures. These drives, irrational, maddening, unreasonable, persistent, are not only urges of the body, they are also urges of the spirit. It is not only that our bodies are fallen — our *nature* is fallen and that means body and spirit. And there is no conquering these enemies or even controlling their hostility except by the grace of God to be obtained through incessant prayer. Why incessant prayer? Because we have incessant drives! That is why we should not stop praying, pardon the expression, until a moment after we have died.

People are not naturally humble. Did you know that? People are naturally proud. Memorize that! Human nature is naturally proud. When you see humility say to yourself "that is grace walking," and it is not a woman's name.

People are not naturally chaste. They are naturally lustful, or as the expression goes, they are *natural*. Amen! So they are! That is what natural means — being lustful! They acquire and maintain chastity only if they pray and pray as much as they need to resist the onslaughts of the flesh.

We are not naturally gentle. We are not naturally selfless. We are not naturally generous or industrious or abstemious, honest.... We are not! My definition of a split second is the time it takes for an empty seat on the New York subways to be occupied. More than once I have stood in front of a person who was sitting and got up. But, supernaturally, I allow the person to get up. I was too late! That is nature — raw human nature.

Left to our own devices we become just naturally, we do not have to work at it, ill-tempered, and greedy and envious and lazy and self-indulgent. Only the grace of God can make us otherwise, and this grace is available only if we pray.

As though that was not enough reason for praying, there is one more malevolent reason why we must pray and that is the devil. Prayer therefore is necessary not only because we are creatures, as we so pathetically are, and because we have a fallen human nature — drop the fallen, we have a human nature — that constantly needs divine grace to keep it...I did not know quite what verb to use...from caving in.

Besides these two so important reasons for prayer, prayer is also and dreadfully necessary because the evil spirit is so active among the sons and daughters of men. No one who sees what is happening in the world today, including what is going on in the Catholic Church, should have any doubt that the devil is more than ever at work in our times and phenomenally successful in leading not just individuals but multitudes, it seems whole nations, away from God. With divine assistance available through prayer we can resist the evil one, but alone and without prayer we shall be overcome.

There are two principles among others to remember in dealing with the devil: first, the devil is by his fallen nature — isn't that good to hear? — the devil, according to his fallen nature, is a consummate deceiver. In fact, another name furnished us by Revelation for the devil is "he is the liar." And, the second principle is that the devil, for all his cunning and deceit, is never allowed to tempt us beyond our strength.

Let us look at each principle separately and see it in the context of prayer. The devil, therefore, is a liar by his fallen demonic nature. He tries to deceive us by presenting what is really evil as though it were something good. He tries to hide his malicious designs behind a mask of piety; or if people are strong on justice, behind a mask of justice, or some other specious claim. Hence, the capital importance of supernatural shrewdness in identifying what may seem to be a divine inspiration but is actually a demonic instigation.

The light we need, however, to cope with the devil we do not naturally possess. We are not naturally smart enough to out-smart the evil one. What we need beyond what we have is the capacity for discriminating between the two spirits of good and evil. And for that we must pray. We need light for many other reasons. But none is more fundamentally necessary than this one: light to recognize the devil, because, leave it to the devil, he will never appear for what he is. He will hide himself behind all kinds of disguises.

Proud persons are no match for the devil. The only remedy for pride is the practice of humble prayer, though I would add besides praying in general, pray in particular. While prayer itself is already an act of humility which God then graces by enlightening us to recognize the evil spirit, we should also, besides, pray for special light to distinguish the devil from the inspirations of grace.

Secondly, the devil is never allowed to tempt us beyond our strength. This means that we always have enough grace to overcome the devil — a long comma; if I stop there that would be an untrue statement.... Is it true to say that we always have enough grace to overcome the devil — period? No! Let's be very clear. No! No period. There must be a comma. We always have enough grace to overcome the devil — comma — provided we have prayed. It cannot be too highly emphasized that when God permits the devil to tempt us — this does not mean that necessarily when the demonic temptation is on us — we already have enough light to recognize him or enough strength to resist him, no less than with other trials in life and surely being tempted by the evil spirit is one of the trials of life. So here we cannot bank on grace already had. We must, absolutely must, pray for additional light and more courage to identify and resist the devil when he assaults us, otherwise, we are liable to give in. Only in this way can we be secure. Hence the transcendent importance of using the word "especially"—that is why God sends us trials—especially to pray when we are tried. That is why we are tried. There's a reason. God tries us precisely that at the moment of trial we might invoke the spirit of light and the spirit of fortitude in order to be able to cope with the evil spirit. Otherwise we run the risk of fighting the devil with inadequate arms and fall victims as so many rash people are being overcome today by this master of deceit.

Let me close with a prayer that I hope thousands of Catholics—let me change the figure—millions of Catholics will once again recite daily to St. Michael the Archangel. How we need God's grace through the intercession of St. Michael today!

"St. Michael the Archangel, defend us in battle. Be our protection against the malice and snares of the devil. Restrain him, O God, we humbly beseech You and do you, O Prince of the heavenly host, by the power of God, drive into hell Satan and the other evil spirits who prowl about the world seeking the ruin of souls. Amen."

We need to pray in order to stay supernaturally alive. We need to pray because we are just creatures and we have been made for God. We need to pray because we have within us desires and fears that we cannot control, only God can. That is why we ask Him to do what we of ourselves cannot do. And we need to pray to cope with the evil spirit who having brought the human race into sin will continue tempting human beings until the end of time, which I like to call the end of temptations. But until the end of our time when we shall have finished our probation we need to pray to be delivered from the evil one.

The Lord's Prayer

When the apostles asked our Lord to teach them how to pray He gave them what has since come to be known as the Lord's Prayer. In teaching them Christ was teaching us, and He taught us many things. My plan is not to give a commentary on the seven petitions of the Lord's Prayer, but rather to reflect in God's presence on the lessons that this prayer should teach us. I choose the following lessons:

—prayer must be taught;
—we should have sacred time for prayer;
—there ought to be togetherness in prayer;
—the God to whom we pray is our Father;
—we ought to have priorities in our prayer;
—when we pray vocally we should understand what we are saying;
—and finally, we should live as we pray.

TEACHING HOW TO PRAY

When Christ was asked: "Lord, teach us to pray," this request was the declaration of a profound truth, namely, that prayer must be taught. This means that in God's ordinary providence we do not precisely know how to pray. We do not know how to pray naturally or spontaneously. We do not know how to pray, I shall not say at all, but, *well*, just naturally. We need grace to know how to pray. We need to pray for the grace to know how to pray. God must be and continually remain our supernatural teacher of prayer so that what the apostles addressed to the Savior as recorded in the Gospels we should often request of Him: "Lord, teach me, teach me *how* to pray. Teach me *when* to pray. Teach me *why* I should pray. Teach me *Whom* I am to pray to. Teach me *what* I am to pray for." Otherwise, quite frankly, we can waste a lot of useful energy unless we pray as we should.

There is such a thing as praying at all and praying well. To pray well we need grace from God; but we also need help from others. We do not know how to pray, well, spontaneously. We need someone to help us. Of all the things that one human being can teach another, there is no science more important than this one. The most needed pedagogy in the world is the pedagogy of prayer. And yet I think none is more taken for granted or neglected. When the Son of God came down to earth He inspired His disciples to ask Him to teach them. On one single occasion they asked Him, "teach us to pray." We assume that people just naturally pray. There is nothing more basic for parents to teach their children; for priests, the faithful; for teachers, their students; and for counselors, the most valuable guidance we can give to anyone is to lead them and teach them how to pray.

SACRED TIME FOR PRAYER

Christ's response on being asked: "Lord, teach us to pray" was "When you pray, say..." and He proceeded to give them—that is, us—the *Pater Noster*. That adverb "when" is precious. It is also very revealing. What was Christ saying? He was in effect saying that there are two kinds of time in our lives. There is what may be called profane time when our main preoccupation is necessarily with creatures, call it secular time. Then there is what may be called sacred time when our main preoccupation is with the Creator.

We cannot physically or psychologically always be preoccupied directly and exclusively with God. That is what heaven is for. There will be no more profane time in heaven. Wonderful! But I do not think that is most people's problem. For most people, they are so preoccupied with creatures that they have little or no sacred time in their lives. They have little or no time for God. Hence the importance of Christ's injunction: "When you pray...." Yes, but that "when" does not just happen, we must make it happen. We must create these "whens" in our lives. No one else, not even God, will do it for us.

When we take time out for God, what bursting creaturely generosity, how nice of us, how thoughtful to take some time out...out of what?...for God. When we interrupt our secular pursuits to think of God. When we turn . . . and it's a turning, there need be no muscular movement, no locomotion through space, but no turning is more active than when we consciously, deliberately and I recommend even bodily, turn. It is a turning all right, from earth to heaven, from time to eternity, and what we embarrassingly must admit, from ourselves to God. But we must want to do it. Those who want those "whens" have them, those who do not, do not. "When you pray, say. . . ."

TOGETHERNESS IN PRAYER

Our Lord made sure that the Lord's Prayer was cast in the first person plural. I counted nine in the English version: *Our* Father; give *us; our* daily bread; forgive *us our* trespasses as *we* forgive those who trespass against *us;* lead *us* not into temptation; deliver *us* from evil.

Clearly, Christ wanted to emphasize the importance of prayer together with others. And no less than creating sacred time, which only we can do, so here too there is an element of consciousness and deliberateness about doing anything with others, including prayer. This can be any one of many forms of togetherness. It can be a togetherness of words when we and others say the same physical prayer. It can be a togetherness of time when we pray together because we pray at the same time (and the sacrifice required in adjusting myself to others and they to me is part of the art of communitarian prayer). Togetherness of place

—we pray in the same room, chapel or church. Togetherness of purpose—when we pray with the same desires and we know beforehand that we are thus praying for the same intention. Togetherness of faith—we all profess because we share the same belief. Togetherness of vocation —when we speak as persons who are at the same time a new moral person called by God to the same vocation. Togetherness of zeal—when what we pray for and how we pray reflects the fact that we are striving after the same goal in the apostolate and realize how God blesses this togetherness of a zealous community.

GOD AS OUR FATHER

When Christ taught us to say the Lord's Prayer He carefully prefixed the word "Our" because when He spoke of His own natural Father He always said, "My Father." The disciples did not ask Him: "Lord, tell us how *you* pray." No, "teach *us* to pray." So "when *you* pray," He said, "say, 'Our Father.'"

The Father, therefore, of the Our Father is the Holy Trinity, Father, Son and Holy Spirit. It is not only and cannot be only the first Person. It is *God* and God is Triune. But, then, we ask: why address God as Father? For the best of reasons, because that is what He is. We are just calling Him by His right name. You see, God is Father in two very different senses as found in the Gospels. He is Father when Christ speaks of His Father, when it is the first Person of the Blessed Trinity; and He is Father in relationship to all creatures, but most especially to the human family. He is then our Father because He made the human race. That is why we are a family! A family has the same parents, except in this case—the same Parent. Remember, when we pray we are speaking to God as members of the same human progeny with a common ancestor who is God.

He is again our Father because He elevated us to membership by grace in His own Trinitarian Family. There is one created family; there is one uncreated "Family." The uncreated "Family"—we have to put the word *Family* in quotation marks—is the Holy Trinity. We have become members by grace of what the three Persons are members by their divine nature.

He is our Father because He cares for us in the two profound senses in which any loving father cares. He cares because He loves, and He cares because He provides. And He provides because He loves. And He would not really be loving unless He also provided.

He is our Father because He has made us heirs of heaven to which only the Trinity has a right. We have no claim on entering the household of God. We have become, thanks to the Incarnation, coheirs with Christ. He is the natural Son; we are the adopted children. But that destiny is still waiting for us. In other words, He not only is our Father now, He will remain our Father for all eternity because then we shall enjoy with Him, and as far as it is possible for creatures, like Him, the beatitude which only the Divine Family of the Triune God has a right to experience.

PRIORITY IN PRAYER

The Lord's Prayer is a series of seven petitions. But they are not casually put together — fancy Christ doing anything casually. They represent three kinds of priorities: the priority of grace over nature; the priority of God's cause over our needs; and the priority of the positive over the negative.

What is the priority of grace over nature? At most two of the seven petitions have to do with temporal, or as we might say, natural blessings: "Give us this day our daily bread," sounds kind of natural, sort of earthy; and "deliver us from evil," and we can think of all kinds of temporal and natural evils. Even these two have primarily a spiritual meaning. But all the others, including these two, are Christ's way of telling us that the main object of our asking should be things of the spirit. First the order of grace and only secondly, or secondarily, things natural or temporal or a nice day tomorrow or relief from whatever pain I may be experiencing... as though pain could not be a grace. So who wants to get rid of a grace? That is the first priority.

The second priority is: God's cause over our needs. If we look carefully over the seven petitions we find the first three refer directly to God and only then do we come down to our own needs. We are up in heaven, "hallowed be Thy name," then "give us this day our daily bread." It is Christ's own expression of His injunction to seek first the kingdom of God and His justice. How we need

to learn this and what a long lifetime it takes, I
do not say to master it, but even to suspect that
it might be so. Provided we look to God's interests first, He will always take care of ours.
How easy to use those words, how hard to live up
to them! If I look to God, God will look after me.

Then the priority of the positive over the
negative. The first four petitions are positive.
Only the last three are negative and Christ
conveniently tucked them underneath. "Forgive
us"—we need remission of our sins. "Lead us
not into temptation," "deliver us from evil."
There are many object lessons, but at least this
one can be mentioned—to stress the positive in
prayer. We are all the same; we are equally
human. We dread this and we fear that. You
cannot imagine the number of things we are
praying...how shall I put it...*from!* "O, Lord,
deliver me." Without excluding that, yet our
primary focus in prayer should be praying for,
though perforce we are perhaps most conscious of our need of prayer when we are in
trouble.

UNDERSTANDING
IN VOCAL PRAYER

Much of our prayer experience is vocal
prayer. Vocal prayer properly explained is
vocal twice over. It is first of all specified words
that are to be said; they are not the spontaneous
expressions of the heart. That is vocal prayer.
Then although vocal prayer could be said in
silence it is also and quite frequently—and when
it is communal, always—said out loud.

The built-in problem with vocal prayer is routine. The trouble with vocal prayer is that it may be vocal all right, but it may not be prayer, or can be so mechanical that the lips are used but the heart can be who knows where. Hence the value of knowing what we are saying when we pray vocally. This I consider the single gravest responsibility we have regarding vocal prayer—to know what we are saying. This makes our prayer more meritorious. It makes vocal prayer more pleasing to God. It makes vocal prayer more what it should be—mental—than merely vocal.

This in turn implies that we periodically meditate on the vocal prayers we recite. There are various methods recommended by the spiritual masters. The essential thing is to take each part of the prayer for separate reflection. So what is wrong with spending an hour on the first two words, "Our Father"? Then beg God even as we reflect to enlighten our minds on the meaning of what we are saying, so that while reflecting we are also asking God: "Lord, what does this mean?" Try to see the prayer as a whole, see how one part is related to another. One of the principal sources of insight in things of the spirit to give us a deeper understanding of God's mysteries is the light that one mystery sheds on another. Things that you have never perhaps seen before will be seen once you relate, for example, the first petition, "hallowed be Thy name" with the last one, "deliver us from evil." You can spend a most interesting three hours in seeing how those two petitions are connected.

It is not, of course, necessary to be actively thinking about the meaning of what we are saying when we are actually praying vocally, but prior meditation will insure that we bring to our lips also our hearts. We shall put into what we are physically pronouncing all that we have learned. What I am saying is that our vocal prayers should always be richer and deeper than just the words we use when we speak. We are to bring all the depth of insight, all the inspiration of soul that by the time we recite the Our Father, the Hail Mary, the...whatever vocal prayer we have by now perhaps said many thousands of times, all that past, all that depth, all that intensity into the words we use when we pray vocally.

LIVING AS WE PRAY

Although we seldom perhaps advert to it, there ought to be a close relationship between our prayer and our life. This relationship should work both ways, from prayer to our life and from life to our prayer. This means, therefore, that our prayer should reflect how we are to live, that we pray for what we need to live as we should, that we pray as God wants us to live.

The Lord's Prayer is the perfect pattern of what our lives should be. They should first of all be lives in which God is first in everything we do, first in intention, first in purpose, first in intensity of effort, first in the time we spend, because even when we are doing other things God should not be totally absent from our minds. It is again the perfect pattern of how we should live because if God is our Father we are His children. The Lord's Prayer teaches us, how eloquently it instructs us, that we are to be and always remain and never dare to rise above being children with respect to God.

Finally, if there is anything the Lord's Prayer teaches us it is the absolute need for humility. What is the Lord's Prayer except the acknowledgment of man's total emptiness before God, his ineptitude to do anything without God? It teaches us that if we live as Christ taught us to pray we shall practice other kinds of humilities, too; but one humility that must be thematic in our life is the sense of our nothingness in the presence of God. We shall learn to live this humility provided we pray as Christ told us when He taught us the Lord's Prayer.

Since the first century of the Christian era the Lord's Prayer has been the most important single prayer in the life of the Church. Its importance in God's eyes must be great because although God became man to tell us many things, there is nothing practically more important than His teaching us how to pray. And it is all locked up in the simple formula of the Our Father.

Understanding the Our Father

There should be no need to apologize for going into a detailed explanation of the *Our Father*. It is the most popular prayer in the Catholic Church. It is the single prayer that all Christians have in common and therefore the one bond of faith on which, at least, we all agree. It is imbedded in the Sacred Liturgy in the Mass and the Divine Office. It is part of every rosary. And for many people it is the one prayer that as believers they most often recite when together as a family or community. It is also the prayer on which more of the saints have written more commentaries than any other prayer in Christendom, going back to the earliest days of the Church. Martyrs like St. Cyprian, theologians like St. Thomas, and mystics like St. Teresa have written in such glowing terms on the *Our Father* as to seem almost excessive. But we know they are not excessive. The *Our*

Father is not only the Church's most important prayer, it is also the most indispensable because it contains the summary of the Gospel and tells us in essence all that is most perfect in the moral teaching of Jesus Christ. For all these reasons there is value in looking more deeply into just what we are saying when we are saying the *Our Father.*

OUR FATHER WHO ART IN HEAVEN...

Our Father who is God is in heaven, and then we must add, and we are still on earth. We are, therefore, addressing God where He is from where we are. We invoke Him in heaven for many reasons. We are expressing the hope that where God is, there too we shall be. We are declaring our faith that there are finally only two realities in the universe, but they are very different and totally distinct:

— the one heavenly, the other earthly;
— the one eternal, the other, thank God, temporal, it is going to come to an end;
— the one divine, the other pathetically, painfully human.

We are, as it were, expressing a sigh, looking forward to being one day totally immersed in that God whom we now only know about. Then we shall see Him and what a difference between seeing a person and knowing a person. Heaven is our home where the Father who made us awaits us, if only we behave ourselves like His children in this world that is so obviously not heaven and, let us remind ourselves, is not meant to be.

HALLOWED BE THY NAME...

This is the first petition of the *Our Father* and what are we praying for? In more simple language we are asking that people should honor God for what He really is, the All-Holy One. It is not, of course, as though this recognition made Him holy. It is rather that being holy His creatures should realize the fact and act on their recognition.

How often we speak of God as holy. So He is. And what does God's holiness mean? It means His total otherness. He is completely not *another* but *the* Other—and you can put a period after that apparently incomplete sentence. He is totally above and beyond and different from everything else that exists. There is no one like God—that is why He is holy. It means that He alone is perfect. He alone is without fault. He alone is sinless. It means that He alone cannot not exist—He alone must be. It means that everyone else, no matter how apparently great, is very small indeed. (How small is nothingness compared to the All.) It means finally that we are to control our natural tendency, and it is a strong one, to praise human beings—especially that one human being, you know who. And exalt first and mainly the name of the Lord, except for whom there would be no other name to praise because there would be no other person with a name. And of all the lavish praise that we give human beings, what we are doing here, betimes, is for a change praising God.

The first petition of the *Our Father* is also the first application of Mary's *Magnificat:* "My soul proclaims the greatness of the Lord." How we need this reminder today when there are so many little people who are proud and there is so much foolish hunger for human praise.

THY KINGDOM COME...

When we pray that God's kingdom might come we imply that somehow it has not yet arrived or not yet been fully attained. That's right! And what kingdom are we talking about? We are speaking of the kingdom of truth, that has not yet conquered (what a safe statement) all the minds of mankind. One glance at the ocean of error in which so many people are submerged tells us there is a vast kingdom yet to establish. We are speaking of the kingdom of love that has yet to take hold of the hearts of men and women in every nation and society. Think of the lovelessness of abortion; of the selfishness of broken vows; or the cruelty of Marxism masking as liberation—and again we see how we need to pray that God's kingdom of love might expand. We are speaking of the kingdom of the Church that Christ founded and that we know, and sadly have to admit, after nineteen hundred years is still not established in many regions of the globe. We are therefore praying that the faithful who already have Christ might share Christ. On that enterprise depends our salvation. Share Him with others through teaching, through preaching, through writing, through the media, but especially through our own lives of holiness that will attract others to follow, provided we portray an appealing Christ. We are speaking of the kingdom of glory to which we are still striving and that we are praying that we and many others will reach when time will end and timelessness begins.

THY WILL BE DONE
ON EARTH AS IT IS IN HEAVEN

This is no ordinary petition. We ask not only that God's Will be done, but that it be done on earth by mortals as it is being done in heaven by the immortal angels and saints.

How is the divine Will being done in heaven? For our purpose as a pattern of how we are to do it on earth. So how is it being done? It is being done by everyone. Imagine! Everyone is doing the Will of God, no exceptions. It is being done constantly, no interruptions. By the way, I hope you know that even when we go to sleep, we are still doing the Will of God. I like the passage: "When my body sleeps, my heart is watching." But constantly in the sense that there are no interruptions — by doing you know who's Will.

It is being done lovingly. That means it is being done just out of love because the people in heaven (which includes the angels) like to do it. And there is no fear. No fear of the possible consequences of not doing God's Will because there is no possibility, won't that be wonderful, no possibility of not doing God's Will. So there cannot be any fear.

It is being done spontaneously, no reluctance. We will not have to make any retreats in heaven to find out what is God's Will and then to motivate ourselves to do it (which is my home-made definition of a retreat).

God's Will is being done selflessly. This is not subtle, but also not obvious. One of the things I have learned in my now thirty years in the priesthood is that there is such a thing as doing God's Will, but you would think, you really would think that we would not be bothered because other people are also doing God's Will. Talk about being strange creatures. Do you know what? We can actually envy other people who are doing good. Did you know that? Astonishing, isn't it? Well, that is earth for you. In heaven God's Will is being done by everyone and no one envies anyone.

One of the hardest things I have found out in such effort as I sometimes expend in working with groups of people, is to get good people to cooperate. How particular they are about who gets credit for what. In heaven, no jealousy.

And finally and best of all, God's Will is being done in heaven enjoyably. Now when we do God's Will there are times, let us be honest— oh, we do it all right, but the effort in muscle or mental exertion makes us, if not sad, at least, not all that happy. We speak of having to do, (is it not true?) God's Will. We still have that word in our vocabulary—"the commandments of God"—with the connotation, "it's something I have got to do." In heaven everyone enjoys doing the Will of God, in fact, that is what the beatitude of heaven is all about—sheer joy in doing God's Will. By the way, lest we forget, we will not just be sitting around. Heaven is active! There will be effort. We will be doing things in heaven. But, all with consummate beatitude.

GIVE US THIS DAY
OUR DAILY BREAD...

At this point, there is a transition from God's interests to our needs. These needs are manifold, but all finally are needs of soul and needs of body. Being alive in either is no assurance of staying alive. In a word, we need nourishment. And the first meaning of this petition is to pray for the food that we need for our souls. What is this food? We need food for the mind which is the Word of God, spoken, written and seen. The human mind starves without the truth and if the deprivation lasts long enough it dies. Food for the will which is the love of God, again, spoken, written and seen. And let us not forget that in large measure we are to be those who communicate this food for the mind and food for the will to others. There must be especially food for the life of the soul because just as the body has its soul, so the soul has its "soul" and the "soul" of the soul is sanctifying grace. That life of grace, no less than the life of the body, must be fed and that food is the Holy Eucharist. St. Pius X in restoring early and frequent Holy Communion to the Catholic world explained that it is the common teaching of the Fathers of the Church that the principal bread we pray for in the Lord's Prayer is "the bread that came down from heaven," the Word of God made flesh in the Eucharist.

What is the food for the body? Again I draw on the Church's now nineteen centuries of wisdom. It is all the means that we and others need for our bodies. It comprehends, therefore, not only food and drink, but shelter and clothing and medicine and therapy and care. What a commentary on the selfishness of so many who possess more than they need when millions do not have enough to eat, no homes, no medical care. Some time ago I was trying to get a young man recently graduated from college into an American medical school. He was from one of the new countries in Africa. I should add he finally got in — it took a long time. I asked him in the course of several conversations: "What is the medical situation in your country?" "Well," he says, "we have four registered doctors for four million people."

Christianity, in my judgment, will be accepted by the non-Christian world when it sees Christians not only saying, but living out this petition of the Lord's Prayer. This is one petition we are in a position to fulfill and we better fulfill it ourselves.

FORGIVE US OUR TRESPASSES AS WE FORGIVE THOSE WHO TRESPASS AGAINST US...

Again, as with the preceding, this is no ordinary request of the Father. We do more here than just ask for mercy from God. We tell Him, listen, we tell Him to measure His mercy to us by our mercy to others. What are we saying? We are telling God that He should be as patient with us as we are with those who cause us pain. That, by the way, is another definition of the virtue of patience. It is willingly accepting pain from others. And people, as we know, can cause us pain in other ways and more painfully than by striking us with a cudgel or cutting us with a knife. Give me a knife any day to some people's speech!

We are telling God that He should be as understanding with us as we are with those who in so many ways are being constantly judged by us before the tribunal of our own minds. To be at least as understanding with others as we are with ourselves. We are telling God to be as long-suffering with us, and that means "long" pause "suffering," as we are with those whom we have to, and we stress the verb, "suffer" — and it may be for no other reason than we do not like, what shall I say, their walk, their talk or the way they take their food.

We are telling God to be as tolerant with us as we are with others, as uncomplaining of us as we are of others, and, as we know by now, the more we have lived with others, by and large, most of us I dare say as we reach adult maturity, learn to avoid open verbal complaint. But, let us face it, it is being uncomplaining about others to ourselves. We are telling God to be as silently ignoring of our weakness, of our forgetfulness, of our boorishness and maybe our downright ingratitude to Him as we are silent in accepting people with their weakness, their forgetfulness, their boorishness and even their downright cruelty and injustice. And the graver the injustice done to us and the worse the cruelty, let me put this in I hope clear theological terms, the more sure we are that one of two things is true. Either we have grave sins to make up for, I'm assuming they have been forgiven, but still to expiate, or God is calling us to extraordinary sanctity. In both cases, God permits people to deal with us in ways that we call offensive. Thank God! This is our principal means of making reparation for our own so frequent and so deep offenses against God. To miss that is to misread Christianity.

LEAD US NOT INTO TEMPTATION...

When we ask not to be led into temptation, we do not ask to be spared temptation. We do ask that the temptation God sends us, that is, permits us to undergo, might not be too much for us. We ask Him to temper the wind to the shorn lamb, that is us. "Lord," we in effect say, "take it easy. You know how much I can take and honestly, You know better than I, it is not much."

We ask that God's permissive temptations might not come at the wrong time. Do you know there are some days when we fear neither man nor beast nor evil spirit? Other days we are just not that strong. And not infrequently, our worst and most humiliating sins have been committed when we were—well—not on our guard. "When we are not feeling even physically so well, Lord, be merciful." We ask God in this petition to take into account our strength and if He is going to send us temptations, "Lord, O dear Lord, be sure to add to the strength that I have which is mainly weakness, so that when I am tempted I will not be overcome."

One little thought about this important petition. We also ask for the light to know what we should do so as not to expose ourselves unnecessarily or unwisely to trials or burdens that would be, as God foresees better than we, more than we could bear. In fact, I would say we especially ask for light. Light not to be overexposed. Light not to take on more than we can take.

BUT DELIVER US FROM EVIL

In the final plea of the *Our Father* we beg the Lord to liberate us from evil. We hear a great deal these days about liberation. Any liberation that is worthy of the name is either circumscribed by this last petition of the Lord's Prayer or it is not the kind of liberation that God wants us to have. What kind of evil are we asking God to be delivered from? Mainly spiritual evil, namely, sin. What we are asking God to do is to make us sinners more and more sinless. We who obviously did not come into the world immaculately conceived, ask through God's mercy that we might leave this world as immaculate as only God's grace can make those who ask for His grace. Our growth in age ought to be progressive sinlessness. After all the complicated words of the spiritual and ascetical vocabulary of the sacred sciences have been read; after all has been disposed of, fundamentally this is it: we become only as holy as we become less unholy. More sinless. And we do not have to read books to know what sins we commit. All we need to do is to daily, and St. Ignatius did several times daily, look into our hearts and read the book of our conscience. Every effort we expend to overcome our sinful

tendencies is "growth in sanctity." How simple!
But I trust you agree — how hard!

Moreover, we ask in this petition to be
delivered from the Evil One, as all the best
Greek manuscripts of the New Testament say
when they give us the Lord's Prayer. They
always end, "but deliver us from the Evil One,"
that is, the devil. We beg God to be delivered
from the snares of the devil. We need this prayer,
all of us, because the devil is especially eager
to seduce. Of course, he wants to seduce all
human beings, but he concentrates especially
on those who are most pleasing to God. It's true.
The holiest people are the most tempted by
the devil. Those who are most important in
the Church. You cannot otherwise explain on any
human terms the tragedy of now tens of thousands
of priests throughout the Catholic world in the
past generation having left the service of the
priesthood except as victims of the devil. Those
who are most influential with others, the devil
concentrates on trying to seduce.

We finally ask to be delivered from such
evils in this world as God knows would not help
us to grow in His friendship. Are we saying
there are different kinds of evil that can befall us? Yes, there are evils which in God's
providence assist us and strengthen us in serving
God. But there are also evils that would not
be for our spiritual welfare. Not everyone
becomes more holy through sickness. Not everyone grows in virtue through opposition. Not
everyone draws closer to God through failure
and misunderstanding. What we especially here
ask for from God is that He spare us such evils
as in His infinite foreknowledge He foresees

would not make us more pleasing to Him. Evils we must experience; this is the valley of tears. We pray that the evils that befall us will be those that sanctify and not those that withdraw us from the God who permits evil not only that good, but greater good might result from the pain or the suffering that evil involves.

Needless to say, the Lord's Prayer is a treasury of divine wisdom, although it takes only a few moments to recite. What God wants us to do is put into those few moments when we recite the *Our Father* all that He intended us to understand when He told us to invoke God as our Father. Our understanding will also be the measure of His generosity to us His children, praying and striving for the heaven where our Father is waiting for us.

The Hail Mary

If there is one vocal prayer that is typically Catholic it is the *Hail Mary*. We say it so many times in different ways, but especially in the recitation of the Angelus and the rosary, and by now must have said it some thousands of times. As we know the present *Hail Mary* is really two prayers, one after the other: the *Hail Mary* properly so-called, and what not too many centuries ago was called the *Holy Mary*. Confessors would tell their penitents to recite, say, three or five or whatever the number of *Holy Marys*. We say it so many times almost subconsciously that if there is correspondingly any one vocal prayer that deserves to be looked at more closely it is this one. My plan is to take this prayer in sequence word for word, or better, term for term, in a prolonged meditation on what its sentiments really mean.

HAIL MARY

This is no casual greeting. It is more than a meaningless "hello" that the angel addressed to Mary at the Annunciation. The best rendition of the word "hail" is "rejoice," "be happy," and it contains a messianic reference to the joy that God had in store for man by becoming Man. It is, moreover, an imperative telling Mary to be joyful, that the dawn of man's salvation was at hand.

The title "Mary" was Mary's before she was so addressed by the angel. It means, among other things, "Lady," corresponding to our English word, "Lord." "Lord" for Christ; "Lady" for Mary. She is then the "Domina" even as He is the "Dominus." It is, in fact, the revealed basis for Mary's Queenship. She was to be the Mother of the Lord of the Universe and therefore the Queen of mankind. One of the most popular devotions in France, I am told, for some time now is devotion to Mary, Queen of the Universe. Makes sense, if her Son is *Lord* of the Universe. That is what the title "Mary" means.

FULL OF GRACE

Our version of the *Hail Mary* is based on the Vulgate translation of the Bible. As you know this translation was done by St. Jerome in the early fifth century on order of Pope St. Damasus I. It is the one and only translation that has been formally approved by an ecumenical council of the Catholic Church. Not only approved, but declared by the Council to be authentic, that is, this translation (I am speaking of the whole Bible, including this passage) contains accurately the substance of God's revelation to man. There are, as by now we know, many other translations of the corresponding Greek words in the New Testament text, for example, "so highly favored," or just, "highly favored," but these translations are merely verbal renditions of the Greek. They do not contain the fullness of doctrinal content that the Church considers to be contained in what is really meant by the words: *gratia plena*.

How, we ask, is Mary "full of grace"? She is full of grace first of all because she was conceived without original sin. Anyone who is in the possession of grace from the first moment of his or her conception would be without original sin. Mary was. Moreover, throughout life she received such an abundance of grace as no one except Christ ever had or will obtain. Again she received grace that not only began her life immaculate, but it kept her absolutely sinless. She remained free from the least even indeliberate venial sin all through life. Then, too, she received grace that kept all her desires totally under control. Unlike the rest of us, Mary had no unruly passions. She had desires, strong desires, but they were always totally submissive to reason under the influence of this fullness of grace. Finally, and most emphatically, she received the unique grace of being invited to become the Mother of the Author of grace. That is quite graceful!

THE LORD IS WITH YOU

This is a direct quotation from the Archangel Gabriel. How, we ask, was the Lord with Mary? He was with her by the grace of His friendship which she enjoyed. Notice the Lord was not only near her or in her, but with her. He was also with her by the faith that she had in what God had revealed about His coming to redeem the human race. St. Augustine, among other Fathers of the Church, tells us that Mary had first conceived God in spirit by faith before she conceived Him in the flesh in her body. It was her deep faith that especially, as far as we can use the language, invited the grace of becoming the Mother of Christ.

The Lord was with Mary, and remained with Mary, by His astounding Providence. God, we should tell ourselves, never gives any grace in isolation. He does not just, as it were, give grace and then walk away. The Lord was with her because He surrounded her with His care and arranged everything in her life to fulfill His providential purpose in her life. But, we should then add, the Lord *was* with Mary, because she was with Him. And this was already before the Incarnation. That "with" implies a conjunction. You are not really with somebody, whatever the preposition means, unless the person is correspondingly also with you.

She, we may safely believe, was always thinking about God. She was also with Him in will. She was always doing what He wanted. She was with Him in heart. As the Evangelists record Mary's speech we do not hear her speaking very often. Yet, on the few occasions when a dialogue is recorded between Mary and her Son, she expresses the most tender, motherly affection. We may be sure she thought of God a lot, she did God's will and she was speaking to Him in sentiments of affection every time she could.

BLESSED ARE YOU
AMONG WOMEN

We turn now from what the angel said to Mary to how she was greeted by her kinswoman Elizabeth at the Visitation. Said Elizabeth: "Of all women you are the most blessed." What does this mean? It means first of all that Mary was unique among all women in becoming a mother without losing her virginity. Mary was unique because she was the Mother of the Messiah. Mary was especially unique among women because the Child she carried in her womb was her Creator. When she gave birth to Christ she could tell Him, or speaking of Him, say: "This is my body," because it was of her that He took on human flesh. So that we teach and we believe: *caro Jesu, caro Mariae*. When God decided to become man He chose to take His flesh of a woman. Surely that Mother was unique.

But Elizabeth does not say merely that Mary was unique among women. That is not what Luke tells us. Elizabeth calls Mary "blessed" which means "happy." This is two greetings of "happiness" in a row, all in the same chapter of Luke—one from the angel, the other from her relative. Our Lady, then, was the happiest of women, in order to reassure us that God wants us already in this life to be happy. And what is the condition of happiness? The one perfectly verified by Mary. It was her humble acceptance of God's will, her submission to His mysterious, and how mysterious, designs.

The greatest problem with God's mysteries is not really that we cannot wrap our finite minds around the infinitely mysterious God; the problem is that some of God's mysteries have to be lived. Mary lived in mystery which means that she lived God's will without ever fully understanding *why.* And the two dramatic occasions when she asked questions — remember? — one at the Annunciation and the other at the finding in the Temple, reveal for all times what we need especially to learn from this happiest of women — *that she walked in darkness. The darkness of faith!* Sure she believed, but that is what faith means — you believe without fully understanding. Mary's joy, therefore, was a result of Mary's conformity to the will of God. Need we add, there is no other means available to man in this valley of tears to be happy. The secret is to do His will without demanding an explanation from God.

AND BLESSED IS THE FRUIT OF YOUR WOMB, JESUS

Elizabeth said not only that Mary was happy, but that the Child in her womb was happy, too. So He was because already in the womb Christ's humanity was substantially united to the Word of God. Already when enveloped in the flesh of His Mother and yet unborn, Christ as Man enjoyed the beatific vision of the Trinity. Who would not be happy in beholding the face of God? Mystics have written eloquently about Christ's hidden life but let us remind ourselves that this hidden life began in the womb. His happiness in this hiding is a lesson for all of us who find being unknown or unrecognized or forgotten so hard to take. Recently in a small gathering of religious when soft drinks were being served, I noticed one of the members of the party was overlooked. He held back for a few minutes, but then you could tell how humiliated and embarrassed he was that just thoughtlessly nobody served him. How human! How real! How we dread to be ignored. How we want, oh how we want, to be known.

But like His Mother, Christ too was doing the will of God. He was happy because He was doing it. Here we touch on the touchstone of the experience of sanctity. No one in his right mind, who has strived well or not so well to do God's will, will deny that that will can be costly, it can make demands on human generosity and self sacrifice. So we ask, what is the compensation? No one does anything unless they get something out of it. What do the great saints and friends of God, what—let us be frank—what do they get out of doing God's will? How I like this passage from Ignatius: "The highest reward that a servant of Jesus should expect in this world from human beings is what his Master received from His own contemporaries: opposition, crucifixion, and death." But does God give something to those who serve Him? Yes! But this yes you do not talk about. This yes you must experience. It is the experience of joy that no one else can give except God and He gives to no one except to those who are doing His will and in the exact measure in which they do it.

HOLY MARY

Mary has many titles in the Litany of our Lady. She has more titles in the churches in

Rome, and still more in the Byzantine Liturgy. I never counted them, but I am told there is a different feast with a different title for our Lady for every day in the Byzantine calendar. Yet this one title, "Holy Mary," has been given to her by the Church because she was the holiest of human beings; she was the holiest of creatures, always after Christ, who is God.

She practiced all the virtues to a sublime degree. She never sinned, but, and I think this bears some emphasis, she was mainly holy not so much by what she did, because as far as we can tell she did not do anything extraordinary; she was mainly so holy because of what she was. She possessed the grace of God. We should emphasize this further, that her holiness was not only because she was the Mother of Christ, indeed, the Mother of God, but because she was in the friendship of God and this kind of holiness we all have access to, and please God, we all possess, trusting that we are in His friendship. This essential sanctity which we share in common with Mary we have because we are in the state of grace.

To be noted, however, is that when we address Mary as holy, we are not only speaking of her holiness *then*. When is that? When she still lived on earth. We are also talking to Mary and addressing her as holy *now*. She is holy because she *now* possesses in heaven a treasury of glory comparable to the fullness of grace she had on earth.

Grace on earth is a condition for glory. The degree of grace is a measure of glory. Though the expression would sound odd, we could legitimately say, instead of speaking of Mary as full of grace, that being now in heaven she is full of glory. She is the most fully glorified of God's creatures, always after her own divine Son. This holiness of our Lady is not only to be praised. It is also to be invoked. She is so powerful in heaven as our intercessor because she is so close to God. The closer a person is to God, the more holy he is. This is another simple word for holiness: closeness to God. Mary is the closest to God. Because she is that close to God, that is, so holy, she is more powerful before the throne of God than any other angel or saint.

Moreover, Mary's holiness is not only to be admired and invoked. It is also to be imitated. She is our model of holiness. She is, as the spiritual writers tell us, the *imitatrix Christi*, the imitator of Christ. Perfect! She is the one who faithfully mirrored His sanctity in the many virtues she practiced. But let us note with Mary, though undoubtedly she practiced the moral virtues of prudence, justice, temperance and fortitude, it was especially her practice of what we call the theological virtue of charity that made her so like Christ in spirit, because she loved Him, who was like her in body, because He was her Son.

MOTHER OF GOD

Already Elizabeth addressed Mary as "the Mother of my Lord." And so the Church has been doing ever since. She was God's Mother because she conceived and gave birth to Jesus Christ who is God, that is why she was immaculately conceived. When God gives a vocation He always plans ahead of time. Knowing that she was to become the

Ark of the Covenant and the first Tabernacle of the Most High, He prepared her body and soul already at her conception. That is also why she was eventually assumed into heaven not only in soul, but also in body. Makes supernatural sense that she might be in the flesh in the company of the Word of God to whom she had given flesh.

This title "Mother of God" is the index of a true faith. By this standard in the early centuries heresy was identified. Those who admitted that Mary was the Mother of God were those who believed that her Son was God. So it has been ever since. Only those, how well I know in dealing for so many years with our separated brethren on their theological faculties, only those really believe in Christ's divinity, who simply and unqualifiedly accept Mary's divine maternity. Anyone who has reservations about Mary being the Mother of God, has reservations about her Son being the Infinite God.

PRAY FOR US SINNERS NOW AND AT THE HOUR OF OUR DEATH

This closing invocation to the Blessed Virgin is at once a confession and a plea. It is a confession that we, unlike Mary, are all sinners. Remember the description of the episodes surrounding the apparitions of our Lady to St. Bernadette at Lourdes when our Lady would recite the rosary with Bernadette? Remember what Mary did as far as Bernadette could tell? She would skip saying the *Hail Mary,* quite correctly. Whatever other reason she had, she could not possibly invoke herself. But most of all she could not possibly call herself what she was not, a sinner. We are! We are, unlike Mary, sinners by inheritance. We have been conceived, let us use the word, "maculately." We have been conceived with a "macula," the stain of the sin that the whole human race except Christ and His Mother, we believe, has inherited.

We are, moreover, sinners by environment. No doubt the society in which Mary lived was in its own way also a sinful society, but unlike Mary we have been not only stained by sin when we came into the world, we have further been stained by the sin of the people around us. We have especially been stained and are sinners by commission, by having offended the God against whom every offense is a sin. We, then, confess that we are sinners.

But besides being a confession, it is a plea. The plea is that Mary might intercede with Christ for us. First of all, now—right now— as we sinners are frightened by the memory of our past sins, as we struggle with ourselves and with others to keep out of sin. One of the hardest things in dealing with people is to keep from becoming entangled in their sins. So we pray that we might be helped now.

We end by asking that we might be protected at the hour of our death. This is our daily and many times daily prayer for final perseverance. Let's be clear in what we are saying. The Church bids us believe that we need to pray for the gift of final perseverance which is not by itself merited even by a lifetime of virtue.

Just because a person has lived a good life does not, by itself, guarantee dying in God's friendship. Over and above this, we must pray for the extraordinary grace that the moment before we enter eternity we receive the gift of dying in the friendship of God. This grace will be given, but not because we have earned it by living a good life. In other words, virtue alone is no promise of dying in the state of grace. We must moreover pray for the grace of a happy death. It is the single greatest grace that any human being can receive. No other can compare with it. And this grace, the Church tells us, must be constantly and earnestly prayed for. That is what we are praying for and confidently hope for because we are asking the Mother of the God who will judge us the moment we die. We are asking her to ask her Son to be merciful. He will be because He loves her. Mary always obtains whatever she wants, provided we have the faith to trust her and the humility to admit our need.

Mental Prayer Is for Everyone

Many people have never heard about mental prayer and among those who have, many could not explain what it is; and among those who could accurately describe mental prayer not all could put it into practice. Even among those who practice mental prayer not all of them, I am sure, profit from its use as well as they could. For all these reasons it seems worthwhile to look at mental prayer as closely as we can so that we might better appreciate what a treasure it really is and appreciating its value might engage in what some saints, like St. Teresa of Avila, have said is absolutely necessary to achieve sanctity. No mental prayer, no holiness. And I would add, it is necessary not only to achieve sanctity, but sometimes even to preserve one's sanity.

What then is mental prayer? Mental prayer can be simply defined. It is the prayer in which the sentiments we express are our own and not those of someone else. Thus understood, mental prayer is actually the heart and substance of all prayer worthy of the name, because even when, as generally happens, the words we use in vocal prayer are those of someone else—of the psalmist, or even of Christ or the Church—we must still somehow make these words our own, appropriate them, and identify ourselves with what we are saying. Otherwise we would be merely pronouncing syllables and not really praying at all. So all vocal prayer must, at least to some extent, also be mental prayer. However, the prayer of which we are here speaking is something more refined. It is that form of prayer in which we ourselves under the impulse of grace make up the words we use as expressions of what is already in our hearts. The degree of this internal expression of our sentiments is a matter of taste or temperament. In essence, however, mental prayer is interior prayer. We interiorly vocalize what is inside of us in such language as we may need to tell God what is in our hearts.

All prayer from the highest raptures of mysticism to the lowly fingering of the beads is a conversation with the invisible world of God, His angels and the saints. As conversation, it is therefore a communion of mind with mind, and of spirit with the spirit world that is unseen by the senses, but ever so seen by the eyes of faith. Whoever said the unseen was unreal? Only the unbeliever!

In mental prayer this conversation has certain qualities that make it distinctive. The conversation with the invisible world is *my* conversation. I do not as such go elsewhere to think of what to say but say what is on my mind and in the depths of my soul. Clearly, this kind of prayer is absolutely distinctive for each person. The conversation is spontaneous. It arises by a kind of heavenly instinct in words and terms of thought that are quite unrehearsed. In mental prayer we are not exactly making a speech to God. Moreover, the conversation is a real dialogue between myself speaking and my invisible Auditor listening. But it also consists of my invisible Auditor speaking and I listening. Mental prayer is not, if it is for real, a monologue. It presumes that as I pray mentally I am both active and passive, both talker and hearer. When I finish any given period of mental prayer, I am to go away enriched in mind and inspired in heart. Mental prayer is a two-way process, from us to the real world of faith, where God and those in His glory abide, and from Him and them back to us who so desperately need their guidance and inspiration. Needless to say, we should give God a chance to talk back. The art of listening in prayer is a fine art.

Finally, conversation in mental prayer is to be an experience. I do not say we must feel in any sensible way the communication between ourselves and the invisible world, but it should be an experience. In mental prayer we are to be, as it were, immersed in what we are doing and involved in our whole being, depending on the degree of intensity we put into prayer and especially on the grace that God gives us when we are in contact with Him and with those who behold Him face to face. Like asking them, how does God look? They should be able to tell us and we should be the wiser for the dialogue.

Mental prayer, we might say, is *total* prayer where the whole of us and not only part of us is consciously and deliberately conversing with God and His friends in glory. You may do other things thoughtlessly or casually — you do not pray mentally without realizing what you are about. We might compare it with the intense conversation we sometimes have with some person about matters that deeply concern either or both of us. There is such a thing as being lost in conversation or of forgetting the passage of time, so intent can we be on what we are saying to the other person and what he or she is saying to us. Again the depth of this intimacy in mental prayer depends mainly on God's grace. But it also depends on us, so much so that we can safely say if we do not more often pray this way the fault is our own. Why our fault? Because being lost in conversation with God in prayer has to be merited. This means it has to be worked at; it means making the effort to concentrate on whom we are speaking with when we pray rather than on ourselves as doing the praying even when, as so often happens, the object of our prayer is our own grave needs.

Who needs mental prayer? There is an easy answer to the question, "who needs mental prayer?" Everybody needs it! Men, women and children need it, the young and the old, the rich and the poor, people in every profession and situation. They need it not occasionally, or only when faced with some overwhelming decision or crisis. They need it always — daily. Depending on their lot in life they may need it often during the day. I speak as one who thinks he needs it often during the day.

In order to make more clear this universal need for mental prayer, let me subdivide the faithful into certain categories — pretty much as the Second Vatican Council classified the People of God in urging all to respond to the universal call to holiness. What are we talking about? We are talking about mental prayer as the indispensable means of reaching sanctity in all the major states of life to which God calls those whom He has sealed in baptism and signed with the confession of the true Faith. No two states of life are quite the same. The needs of one are not the needs of another, and the responsibilities of one are not precisely those of another.

One of the pities of our age is that so many people are trying to live other people's lives. Call it role-playing or personality-substitution or dissatisfaction with one's state of life. Whatever the name, it is a phenomenon that should be given more attention than it is getting with all sorts of shifting of life's goals until Western society is writhing with a massive confusion which this instability has created. It is almost as though there were no states of life. Everybody seems to want to be somebody else. So many women behaving as though they wanted to be men; men as though they were women; husbands as though they were not married; and wives as though they had no husbands or families; priests as though they were businessmen, politicians or social activists; and religious as though they were secular men and women in the world. Consequently, when we speak of everyone needing mental prayer this means that everyone needs a certain amount of regular reflection in God's presence and in conversation with Him in order to be what God wants him or her to be.

The subject we are entering, and we shall soon have to leave it, is a panoramic one but at least we can take a bird's eye view of what this concretely means. There are in the main, five states of life recognized by the Church as being distinct. One is not the other, even when some person may perchance span more than one of these states in his lifetime.

There are, then, five states of life—each a special calling from God. And each calls for its measure of mental prayer from the person who wishes to live out his or her vocation and not someone else's, according to the will of God. There are bishops and priests and religious and the married and the single, whether married before or not. Each has been established by the all-wise Governor of the human family. Each has its own corresponding duties, that in God's Providence cannot be adequately fulfilled or even lived up to unless each according to his respective vocation practices daily mental prayer. The content of their mental prayer will be different for the simple reason that their vocations are not the same.

Suppose we briefly identify in a quick glance the principal duties of these five principal states of life. Clarity here is necessary if the graces that God intends to give each will be given according to each one's needs. We shall obtain what we ask for, so we had better ask for what *we* need — underline, block off, "what we need," which implies that we know what *we* are supposed to be and do according to *our* call from God. In every case we shall single out only two distinctive duties for each divine vocation, while recognizing that every state of life has many other duties besides.

What are the principal duties of bishops in the Catholic Church? The principal duties of bishops in the Catholic Church are to teach the faithful the truths of revelation and to lead the people in the ways of God. Every bishop should be a teacher and a leader of the People of God. There is no single greater need in the Church today.

What are the principal duties of priests? The principal duties of priests are to sanctify the faithful by their consecration of the Holy Eucharist and to mediate God's mercy through the forgiveness of people's sins. Every priest, therefore, should be Christ's instrument in bringing the Eucharist among the faithful and in reconciling them with an offended God. No priests — no Eucharist! If we have grave sins, God wants us to submit them, as we say, to the "power of the keys" in sacramental confession. And if we wish to grow in sanctity, even though we do not have grave sins, we must frequently use this sacrament, strange to say it, of sanctification which only priests can administer.

What are the principal duties of religious? The principal duties of religious are to witness to God's holiness by their consecrated lives and to communicate God's goodness by their service to mankind. The witness of sanctity and the generous meeting of people's needs should characterize a true religious. Religious are to be professionals in professing sanctity. Because of their life of consecration they should be free both physically (in time and energy) and spiritually (in selfless detachment) to devote themselves entirely to the service of their neighbor.

What are the principal duties of the married? The principal duties of the married are to co-operate with the Creator in begetting children and training them to serve God, and to testify to God's fidelity by their own unfailing love. Married people, therefore, are to bring new life into the world and nurture this life in body and mind. And they are to reflect the constancy of Christ's love for His Church and of God's love for the world by their own unswerving devotion to one another and to the offspring they may have.

There are many reasons why so many people have lost their faith in God. Among the reasons, I believe, is the fact that so many married people have so poorly reflected what should be present in their married lives. They do not see enough love and stability and generosity among God's creatures to even *reason* to the fact that there is an all-loving, infinitely generous and un-changeable God. Our reason and faith must be supported in the world in which we live in order to continue strong in recognizing the attributes of God.

What are the principal duties of the single? The principal duties of single people are to use their independence and resources for the welfare of other people and to show by their chastity the power of grace over fallen human nature. Having a true vocation, single people in the world are to spend themselves for others in works of charity and they are to inspire the secular culture in which they live with the beauties of Christian chastity.

All of these responsibilities in the main states of life recognized by the Church must be sustained by assiduous mental prayer. Mental prayer is necessary even to recognize one's own vocation as distinctive from that of others. It is necessary to maintain one's commitment to a definite choice, once and for all made. It is necessary to remain faithful in one's special calling from the Lord. How few — better, how none — who when they enter on a state of life could possibly foresee all contingencies that this life will bring. Mental prayer is necessary to resist the temptation to discouragement or to needless change, forgetting what St. Paul tells us, that the particular way in which the Spirit is given to each person is for a good purpose. But I must see that purpose. To resist the temptation to change from what I have been to what I might be — I need prayer.

There is no problem so grave in any state of life that cannot be resolved through humble mental prayer. But there is also no problem so small in every vocation that cannot become an impassable jungle in the absence of mental prayer. Mole hills become mountains or, as I watch the ants working along the pathway, ant hills become the Rockies, unless through daily mental prayer we keep our perspective.

"Holy Spirit," we need pray, "teach me to pray in such a way that I shall find joy in my chosen way of life. Teach me to respond to the responsibilities of my vocation with a generous heart, seeing that there is a variety of gifts but always the same Spirit, that is, You."

"There are all sorts of service to be done but always the same Lord working in all sorts of different ways in different people," para-phrasing the Apostle quoting the Holy Spirit.

To know the particular way the Spirit wants to work in me and to have the courage to let Him do what He wills is the main purpose of mental prayer for everyone. It is also the surest means of achieving peace, when I know that I'm doing the will of God.

Practical Meditation

Meditation is the most popular form of mental prayer and is the normal way that persons in whatever state in life sustain themselves in their respective commitments to God. Sometimes meditation is distinguished from contemplation, and there is theologically a difference, but, I think, it is more a matter of degree than of kind. In meditation our mental prayer is and should be contemplative, but the activity of the mind predominates. In contemplation our mental prayer is meditative. It has to be, but the activity of the will and the affections predominate. Our focus here is much more specific. We wish to look at what I call practical meditation in the sense that meditation is primarily directed to living out in practice, hence practical, the state or way of life to which we have been called.

All meditation in one sense is practical even when the object of our mental prayer is, say, a mystery of the faith like the Incarnation, or the Holy Trinity, or a mystery of Christ's life, like the institution of the Holy Eucharist, or a passage from the Scriptures like verses from the Psalms. But the practicality we envision here is the down-to-earth putting into praxis what our distinctive vocation in life demands. My intention in this conference is to do one thing: help to make our meditations more meaningful because hopefully we shall better understand what they are all about, speaking of such meditations as concern God's will in our daily lives.

What should we hope to get from these practical meditations? We should obtain certain blessings from God as the fruit of our mental prayer which is mainly petitional. These blessings will not necessarily come in this order and not necessarily all at once, but we may expect at least the following:

We should come to know better who we are. The law of the spiritual life is that it is built on two forms of knowledge, the knowledge of God and the knowledge of self. Here, then, our first purpose should be to know better who *we* are.

We should come to learn what is our personal responsibility according to our state of life. Others have their problems. If you want as a matter of spiritual recreation to meditate on other people's problems once in a while go right ahead. We are here discussing, reflecting on what are *my* responsibilities in my own vocation.

We should better understand *why* we are to do what our vocation demands. I have more than once had occasion, for example, in a dentist's or doctor's office for a half an hour or longer to watch the dialogue between a young child and its mother: "Why this, why that?" Questions that no one, and certainly not the editor of the magazine, could have dreamt would be asked: "Why this color?" "Why the horse?" We never cease to be children. We always need to know *why* in the spiritual life.

We should become clear about *how* we are to meet our responsibility here and now. Some people specialize in what I call futuristic meditations. "How am I supposed to do what I am supposed to do, like this morning, or the next hour?" This kind of practicality I have learned from dealing with many souls. When we pray, let us be sure to ask the Lord how to meet, or cope with, or deal with what is facing me here and now.

And finally we should be able to leave mental prayer stronger in virtue to fulfill God's manifest will in our regard. The first four parts will insure the manifest will, but manifest will is not enough. We must also have the will power to meet this manifest will of God. You get it by asking for it.

SELF-KNOWLEDGE

The first fruit of mental prayer as practical meditation should be a better knowledge of ourselves, not so much as an individual with a particular name, but as a person with a particular calling from the Lord. This kind of self-appraisal is not easy to come by. Books and conferences and counsel from others may help, but Christ Himself, the Master who dwells in our minds by His grace, must further teach us.

Why ask Him for light to know ourselves vocationally—to coin a strange adverb? Otherwise the trials of our state of life can pile up and the difficulties to be borne can become so heavy that we are liable to give up, if not entirely, at least we can slip into a comfortable mediocrity and scarcely walk in the paths of holiness expected of our calling instead of running ever upward and onward on the road of sanctity.

Father Faber, a great spiritual writer, spoke of weariness-in-well-doing. I like that. There is such a thing as just getting tired of being good. There is also another reason why the first and enduring purpose of mental prayer should be to keep us minded of who we are; otherwise we shall start thinking foolish thoughts about the "might-have-beens" in our life. We are liable to lapse into a dream-world of our own fantasy where the grass on the other side of the fence looks greener, or where the roses in someone else's garden seem to have no thorns. So instead of settling down to being what we should be, minding our own business—a good priest, a good religious, or a good parent—we begin living in an unreal world that looks more pleasant and less unpleasant than the real world to which we have been called.

There is no easy calculation of the percentage of fiction works among the books published and read compared to all the other published literature put together. A calculated estimate, however, is that over 90% of people's reading in the literate world is fiction. This may tell us many things. To me it symbolizes the desire of so many people to escape reality. Some use fiction, some use drugs, some take to drink. It is not enough, however, to tell ourselves, "Stop daydreaming, come down to earth, face reality." We need the constant influence of divine light assured only to those who pray for it, to keep our imagination under control and our desires submissive to sound reason and faith.

PERSONAL RESPONSIBILITY

Here is another "not enough." It is also not enough to know who we are whatever our state of life may be. We must also learn what our personal responsibilities in this way of life really are. After all, being, say, a priest is one thing; it is something much more and further necessary to know what *this* priest, namely myself, is expected to be and do. The definition of the priesthood as found in sound books of theology can be expressed in a sentence or two. But no sentence, no thousand sentences, can exhaust all that this one single priest with these qualities and limitations should be doing. What book do you read? What counselor do you consult? And so of all the other states of life.

To bridge the gap between theory and practice one must pray and pray earnestly, again for light from the Spirit of Light, to tell me what *I* am supposed to do. That is why I was so pleased when Archbishop Sheen, on my visit to his apartment in Manhattan, told me

(He led me into his private chapel with the Blessed Sacrament and said), "This is where I do most of my work." So I told him frankly, "That is where I do most of my best work, too, though I do not have a private chapel." Most of my thinking, most of my planning and a lot of my writing. "Lord, what do I say next?" And some times He tells me: "I will not tell you. Come back." So I come back.

It is remarkable how many theoreticians, say of child care, are hopelessly impractical in guiding their own children and training them properly. As one mother told me about her daughter—babysitter, babysitting for a nationally renowned child-psychologist. She said, "My daughter tells me she has babysat, if that is a verb, for many families. None in all her experience were more difficult to control, more unruly, more impudent, than the little dears of that nationally known child-psychologist."

Or, how many speculative writers on the religious life have made a shambles of their own once-dedicated life to God. The prayer addressed to the Savior: "Lord, that *I* may see" is profoundly true, provided you place the accent where it belongs. I must see *me* and not some third person in the role of whatever under God I now am. Otherwise, I may be applying someone else's norms of moral behavior to myself and no wonder I will fail miserably in the process.

SUSTAINED MOTIVATION

I need further help from God to enlighten me constantly on why I should be doing what evidently He wants me to do. This again is not so easily come by. Remember we are talking about lifetime commitments which imply a lifetime of unpredictable events and mistakes, and perhaps an occasional tragedy. If I have to remain constant in my commitment and not waver in my original willingness or generosity, I have to be—the word is, *have* to be—supported constantly by strong sustained motivation in my will which itself is sustained by reasons why.

Some of the great modern masters of spirituality put this down as the main single reason why some people, otherwise holy, good persons, do not achieve great things as far as we can humanly tell. What they lack, so it is said, is the strong motivation that it takes to keep one afloat in what perhaps in a burst of fervor I may have undertaken. As time goes on those original reasons may be fewer than when I was first ordained, or married, or took my vows. But the number of reasons is not important. And I would say we cannot even live on yesterday's motives, let alone those of ten or twenty years ago. I need motivation today. One of the blessed fruits of mental prayer is the grace we receive to purify our motives and maybe, and here is one person who has, discard a few. I would hate to tell you publicly some of my reasons for joining the Society of Jesus.

Under divine influence we shall become more selfless in our fundamental reasons for being and continuing what one day, it seems so long ago, we had told God we wanted to be for the rest of our lives. Not only will our motives become more pure under the purifying light of God's grace; through prayer they will also become more supernatural as time goes on, provided we have faithfully prayed for the light which now becomes "Lord, that I may see *why!*"

HOW TO FULFILL MY DUTIES

Yet one more insight, and for our purpose, grace, is constantly needed from the mind of God to our mind if we are not to fail in living up to our state of life. This is the grace, to coin a fancy term, of methodology; a big phrase to identify a crucial part of becoming what God wants us to be. It is not enough, for the third time, as we now well know from experience, to conclude that we should be whatever our vocation demands — more prayerful, or more patient, or zealous, or generous than we obviously are. We also have to know how. There are any one of a thousand duties to be actually carried out. I am a bishop in whose diocese some priests are taking such liberty with the liturgy as to be a grave scandal to the faithful. How should I cope with the situation, at once faithful to my responsibilities as ordinary of the diocese and prudent in not perhaps creating a worse situation if the matter is not handled carefully?

I am a priest in whose parish are some persons who evidently resent my authority, say in teaching sound doctrine to the children or insisting on proper decorum in church. How should I deal with these persons or others in similar situations? Or how even deal with some one person who has become a cross in my life? Only God with His enlightening grace to be sought in meditation can give me the help that I need.

I am a religious who wants to live up to the clear directions of the Church in my consecrated life. But there are persons perhaps close to me in my own community who have a different philosophy. How to act? What to do? Where to turn? No matter whom else I consult, my principal counselor, and not once but almost constantly, must be the Savior who called Himself the Light of the world and who will certainly enlighten my own little world to teach me how.

I am a parent whose child or children have reached a point where I sometimes wonder if I have any authority left in the family. As long as I live I shall never forget the couple and their 15-year-old son that I was counseling. At one point in the conversation this strapping young man — when his father was talking to me — kicked his father and told him, "I told you to shut up." The parent may say, "I have discussed the matter maybe many times with my husband or wife, with my confessor, with who knows whom." But in today's confused world no parent can make it without something more. I must regularly discuss my problems as a father or mother with the Lord who dwells within me. I must ask His advice and listen to His directives, because without Him I will only painfully know the problem but remain blind as to what to do and how to do it.

I am a single person, man or woman, and I honestly believe that God wants me to remain as I am in the world and unmarried. But how? There are so many seductions all around me — so many people who seem not to care. Or, as one group of single women to whom I was giving a weekend conference told me: "Father, we wish you could do something about it. Listening to the prayers, there are prayers for fathers, there are prayers for mothers, there are prayers for priests, there are prayers for religious, prayers for children. Would you please ask people to pray for us?"

There are so many options they say that lie ahead of me. So many pitfalls to avoid, and opportunities I would like to take, but how? How serve others and keep myself wisely detached? How remain chaste in a jungle of sexuality? How be in the world and not become worldly? By now I have told many, "Whatever counsel I can give you, you need constant daily mental prayer."

One of the many satisfying experiences that I have had is the counsel that a very success-ful medical practitioner has put into practice. The first thing he does after he gets up in the morning before the rest of the family is to spend a half hour in mental prayer. I think priests and religious should talk this language to more peo-ple, and children should be introduced to the first beginnings of easy, and for them spon-taneous, talking in their own language with the God who dwells in their hearts.

SPIRITUAL STRENGTH

There is one more practical need, or for our purpose, practical fruit of meditation and it is in a way the most important. It is strength to carry out what God wants me to do. After all, it is one thing to know who I am, what are *my* responsibilities, why I should do them. I may even know how they are to be done. It is something else and more to have what it takes to do what I am supposed to do.

Spiritual writers are now talking in a way that is a bit unusual about grace. They are speaking of the grace of enablement, or the grace of empowerment. The language may be a bit odd, but the truth behind the words is not odd at all. What does it mean? It means that the main fruit of practical meditation should be just that: the practice of my duties in my vocation because I have received and continue receiving the enablement from God to do what of myself I could never do. It is not quite correct to say that God never commands the impossible. The impossible that God commands may mean the impossible that I cannot do without adequate grace. And God does not guarantee *ipso facto*, automatically, or inevitably all the grace we need to do what He wants me, what is my duty to do, as whatever I am—bishop, priest, or religious, mother, father, or single person in the world. It may indeed be impossible, and God is not unjust because, having told me, "Do this," He also told me, "Pray for what you lack. And unless you pray, then do not blame me for being unable to do what you are supposed to do." I cannot exaggerate the importance of this principle of the spiritual life.

Shortly before His ascension, and in fact just before He left this earth to return to the Father, the Savior told the disciples, "You will be given power when the Spirit comes on you." This is one of the most practically important statements of revelation. But, and listen, listen— what did He tell them to do before that Spirit of power would come? He told them to pray! That promise, but also that condition was not only for the disciples in the first century; it is the promise and proviso for all of us today. The promise is power; the proviso is prayer. We must ask, God will give, but only if we ask for the strength that we do not have and therefore we need. God wants to make sure that we do not lose sight of the fact that we need His help. Oh, He is shrewd! How shrewd! He keeps us always in a begging posture. That is why He puts into every vocation such trials and difficulties as only God's grace can cope with or overcome.

That is the way it is! More than we can do, but do not stop the sentence, of ourselves. St. Paul had no doubt about his vocation. He was an apostle born, he admitted, out of due time; but he told the whole wide world he was an apostle of Jesus Christ and let no one doubt his claim. But, being an honest man, he also knew how weak and unequal he was to the task laid upon him. No one in all the annals of spiritual literature has better expressed this disproportion between divine calling and human capacity, between God's demands and man's inability. What he said he should do he was inclined not to do and what he should not do his whole nature clamored for, until he begged in supernatural desperation, "Who will save me from the body of this death?" His answer is our answer: the grace of Jesus Christ.

One truth, then, that we cannot forget about, the grace of vocation is that when God calls He also assures those whom He calls the grace they require to fulfill the heavy expectations that God has of them. Yes, the grace will come, but *not*—do not forget that negative— not without the asking. Graces will come in abundance and such power as only the Almighty can give, but we must humbly, constantly and confidently lay our needs before Him in practical meditation. Leave it to God to do the rest. He always does.

Prayer and Suffering

Christianity is unique among the religions of the world in giving a rational and adequate explanation of suffering. In fact, it goes beyond giving an explanation; it gives its followers a strong motive for suffering. This motive being the fact that God became man in the person of Jesus Christ. Those who love Christ are to love the whole Christ, the child of Bethlehem and the naked, condemned criminal on Calvary, the Christ in the manger and the Christ on the cross. Those who love God, therefore, on Christian terms, do not or should not run away from suffering. If anything they expect it and for nineteen centuries they have not been disappointed. In every age and at every stage of their passage through time, the experience of Christians has been a share in the experience of Christ which includes joy and peace, of course, but also and emphatically includes suffering.

Our focus in the present reflections, however, is more particular. We wish to look at two cardinal mysteries of the Christian faith to see how they are related and what light each sheds on the other: the mystery of prayer and the mystery of suffering.

What is Christian Suffering? We begin then by looking at what may seem plain enough on the surface, but is not as plain as many people think, namely, just what is suffering? If there is one thing that everybody experiences but few people define, it is suffering. As commonly understood, suffering means the experience of pain. It may be, and for many people it is, mainly bodily pain due to a variety of causes. Every organ of the human body, every limb and every joint, in fact, every cell is capable of greater or less, and at times excruciating, pain.

So great is the horror of bodily pain that annually billions of dollars in our country are spent by those who can afford it to avoid pain or lessen pain. And every drugstore is a symbol of man's dread of pain and his desire to be relieved of bodily suffering. But there is pain not only in the body. It is not just our body that suffers, it is *we*. There is also pain in the human soul. To be rejected by those we love is pain. To be misunderstood and worse still to be misrepresented is pain. To be passed over when others are chosen, or ignored when others are recognized and praised, or forgotten when others are remembered, is pain. To have strong desires, noble desires like union with God and a sense of His nearness, and not have these desires fulfilled, as the mystics tell us, is great pain. To make mistakes and as a consequence be embarrassed, or to do wrong, then have to live with the memory of our sins, is pain. So the litany of pain goes on and its experience is suffering.

But Christian suffering is not the mere experience of pain, nor even just the tolerance of pain. In the Christian philosophy of life suffering is to be sanctified and the sanctification of suffering is called sacrifice. It took me twenty years to reach that definition. I share it with you.

Every human being suffers, some more and others less, but all have to undergo pain. But sadly and most tragically, not everyone sanctifies his suffering to make it a sacrifice. And it is here that Christianity has so much to teach the world. In fact, so much to teach Christians. So we ask: how do we sanctify our sufferings such as they are and change them by divine alchemy into sacrifice? We do so through the mysterious power of prayer.

What do I do when I suffer prayerfully? Now that is a new term, I suppose. When I suffer prayerfully I do many things but especially these:

First, I see that behind what I endure is not the person or the event or the mishap or even the mistake (as obvious as these may be). I acknowledge that the real active agent responsible for my suffering is the mysterious hand of God. When David on one dramatic occasion, while on the road, was being insulted by a certain Shimei who cursed the king, called him a scoundrel and an usurper and began to throw stones at him, David's armed guard exclaimed, "Is this dead dog to curse my Lord, the King? Let me go over and cut off his head!" But David would not let him. "Let him curse," he replied.

"If Yahweh said to him: 'Curse David,' what right has anyone to say 'why have you done this?' Perhaps Yahweh will look on my misery and repay me with good for his curse today." Unquote: David, inspired by Yahweh. First, then, when I suffer prayerfully I recognize that God is behind the suffering and I humble my head in faith.

Second, when I suffer prayerfully I trust that God has reasons for permitting what I endure and that in His own time and way, the experience now suffered will eventually somehow be a source of grace. What David did in the Old Testament, Christ, the Son of David, not yet born, enabled him to do by anticipation because of the mystery and the merits of the Cross. If ever we are tempted to doubt the value of suffering patiently, according to the will of God, we have only to look at the Crucifix. Talk about value in suffering! But the value derives not from physical or spiritual pain. It comes from the Infinite God who showed us — this is God teaching us — who showed us by His own passion and death how profitable prayerful suffering can be. The most important single lesson mankind had to learn — the meaning of suffering and its value. It took God to teach us. And He had to resort to the extreme expedient of becoming man and suffering Himself to prove to us that suffering is not meaningless; that it is not valueless; that undergone prayerfully, it is the most meaningful and valuable experience in human life.

For reasons best known to the Almighty, once sin had entered the world, grace was to be obtained through the Cross, which really means, through the voluntary acceptance of God's will crossing mine. This voluntary acceptance on our part is what the Father required of His Son as the condition for opening the treasury of His mercies. It is still the condition today for conferring these blessings on a sinful mankind.

Suffering elevates prayer. No one who understands even the rudiments of Christianity should doubt that prayer is necessary for every believer if he wants to be saved. It is further well known that progress in virtue and growth in holiness depend absolutely on fervent and frequent prayer. What is perhaps not so well known is that prayer has interior depths that are not exactly the same as having mystical experiences or having ecstasies or even going through what some of the great friends of God, as Francis of Assisi or Catherine of Siena received from the Lord—those are depths (though I suppose, more accurately, are heights of prayer). We are talking about depths. These interior depths of prayer are not the phenomena that some people mistakenly take to be God's special presence and evidence of the miraculous diffusion of His gifts. The depths of which I am speaking are those of the souls in love with Christ the Savior in prayer, when this prayer is joined with suffering willingly undergone or even willingly undertaken as evidence of a generous heart.

There is a passage in the writings of St. Ignatius that I almost hesitate quoting for fear of having him misunderstood. The saints sometimes said strange things. But it is worth the risk in order to make more clear what I think is so much needed today to protect people from what I consider the heresy of instant mysticism.

When all sorts of fads and gimmicks are being sold to the faithful as means of becoming holy or of discovering "their oneness with the Absolute," I quote St. Ignatius:

"If God gives you an abundant harvest of trials, it is a sign of the great holiness to which He desires you to attain. Do you want to become a great saint? Ask God to send you many sufferings. The flame of Divine Love never rises higher than when fed with the wood of the Cross, which the infinite charity of the Savior uses to finish His sacrifice. All the pleasures of the world are nothing compared with the sweetness found in the gall and vinegar offered to Jesus Christ. That is, hard and painful things endured for Jesus Christ and with Jesus Christ." Unquote: my father and guide, St. Ignatius.

We may object that these are the sentiments of a great mystic who, as all mystics, spoke in symbolic terms and is not to be taken literally. Not so. They are the prosaic words of all those who believe that the most pleasing prayer to God is the one that proceeds not only from the lips or even only from the heart but one that comes from the heart indeed, but a heart that is suffering in union with the heart of the innocent Lamb of God. Not all the faithful are called to the heights of this kind of prayer, although no Christian is exempt from his share in the life of the Master whose prayer to His Father was so efficacious because it was constantly elevated by the Cross.

Other things being equal, the more my prayer life is crucified, the more meritorious it becomes. The more what I say to God is combined with what I offer to God, the more pleased He will be. The more my petitions to the Lord are united with sacrifice willingly made, the more certainly what I ask for will be received. There is such a thing as cheap prayer. I call that comfortable prayer. There is such a thing as dear prayer. I call that sacrificial prayer. I don't know where the idea came from that the essence of prayer is, well, just praying and, presto—we have satisfied our prayerful duties and can go on to other things. Not at all. Prayer is an ongoing enterprise and its continuance is especially prolongation of what I say to God (which may not be much) with what I endure and suffer for God (which can be very much).

Peaceful endurance through prayer. We still have one more reflection on our general theme of prayer and suffering that should not be omitted. How to maintain one's peace of soul while undergoing whatever trial God may send us? This is no trivial question because for failure to answer it—either at all or at least satisfactorily—I am afraid that many otherwise good people do not grow to the spiritual stature that Providence intends for them and certainly do not accomplish in their service for others all they could.

What are we saying? We are asking ourselves—each one—a very special question. How can I live up to the sublime teachings of my faith and suffer as God wants me to without becoming anxious, worried and irritable in the process? Christ could not be plainer in telling me to bear the Cross; He could also not be plainer in telling me not to worry, but to be at peace. The problem is: how do you combine the two? How can I practice the one—

that is, carry the Cross; and maintain the other—
that is, be at peace? I am afraid that sometimes
God, after having sent us some splinter of the
Cross, almost tells us: "Well, if that's the way
you feel about it...all right, all right, no more
Cross, at least of that kind, for you. I can see
you can't take it." The answer on how to combine the two is the prayer of sacrifice.

We begin by admitting, without delusion,
that suffering means suffering and there is
no disguising the fact. But there are two sides
to every painful experience—there is objective
pain and there is my subjective reaction. The
same objective source of pain—say a cut or a
wound in the body, an insult or humiliation in
the soul—can produce only a mild reaction in one
person and invoke a delirium of agony in another.
Or even the same person, on one occasion is
not much disturbed over the painful experience
he has, and at another time, feels it excruciatingly
or worries and can worry himself sick over some
future suffering with convulsive fear. Our
interest here is not to know how psychologically
to cope with the trials of life so as not to suffer
more than we should; it is rather to see how
we can preserve ourselves in peace whenever
God's hand touches us, or He asks us, as He
does, to carry our Cross.

The method, we said, is through the prayer
of sacrifice. What does this mean? It means
that whenever any trial enters our life, no
matter how small, we prayerfully place ourselves in God's presence and voluntarily accept
the trial. Memorize that. We prayerfully place
ourselves in God's presence and *voluntarily
accept* the trial. I said we should do this no
matter how small the trial may be, and one index

of how big we are or how grown-up spiritually is the little things that can rock us. After all, most of our difficulties are not individually major problems and there is great wisdom in spelling them out and dealing with each one as it comes. That's a side issue, just to mention it: one trial at a time. These trials can be humiliatingly small things taken separately but together they can become oppressively big.

A priest confrere of mine tells the story of a pilgrimage he once attended and how during the pilgrimage he shared his room with another man. The priest said, "Hardly had my partner gone to bed than he began to snore loudly, loud enough to waken the dead. At first I started to be impatient, then I applied the remedy— I willed to listen to the snoring and hear it clearly, tranquilly observed it and, a little later, fell asleep. Waking up once during the night (the noise was terrific!), I used the same method again and returned to sleep."

There are in the lives of all of us countless sources of annoyance—all kinds of noise and distasteful persons, places and things. We can be opposed or oppressed but we should never be depressed by no-matter-what tribulation enters our lives. The way to retain our peaceful serenity is to promptly ask God to endure what cannot be changed or in His own time to change what for the time being is to be endured. What God wants of us is a pure sacrifice unalloyed by our reluctance to suffer at His hands or made worse than His Providence intends. What He wants us to endure is all the pain that He wants to give us, being sure He will never give us more than we can bear. What He does not want is to have us spoil the opportunity for sacrifice by making an issue of what is, after all, the normal way He deals with those whom He calls His friends. This is God's way of embracing those that He loves. What God wants is that we, by resigning ourselves to His gracious will, may do His will — which can sometimes be hard but always it is to be done in peace. This is what Christ must have meant when He told us: "My yoke is easy and my burden light." Surely, serving God does mean carrying the yoke and the burden that He sends us. The secret is to see in prayer that they are *His* yoke — oh, those important pronominal adjectives: *my* yoke, *my* burden. He wants us to prayerfully realize that they are *His* yoke and *His* burden that *He* places upon us, and let us be sure that is plenty and for that we have the grace. If we can keep this vision before us through life, we shall not, of course, be spared the Cross — that would be unthinkable — but we shall be at peace. Peace is the absence of conflict between wills, here between the will of God and ours. It is open to everyone who is willing to pray and live by His prayer: "Lord, not my will but Thine be done."

Praying the Mass

I doubt if any single aspect of the Catholic Church since the Second Vatican Council has caused more confusion and worry among the faithful than the Eucharistic Liturgy. From many parts of the Western world come reports of not a few Catholics who have simply stopped going to Mass, others who insist on having the Mass celebrated only in Latin and according to the Tridentine Ritual. How many times I have been seriously asked by people whether the present celebration of Mass in the vernacular and following one of the new canons was valid. I have heard of people walking out of Sunday Mass, and there are movements and publications crusading for a return to the pre-Vatican liturgy and some even daring to question the authority of the Second Vatican Council because it sanctioned what these people call a betrayal of Catholic liturgical piety.

It is not my purpose here to go into a diagnosis of what happened, nor do I think all the blame is on one side. There have been so many liberties taken with the ritual, so many subjective interpretations of the Council's teaching, so many emotional substitutions for what the Church has clearly prescribed, so many intrusions of the secular into what should be the sacred functions of the Mass, that, without excusing those who are anguishing or angry with the post-conciliar liturgy, we can at least partially explain their conduct as a reaction to the grave abuses that the Holy See has more than once condemned in the most unmistakable terms.

All of this I thought is useful to bring to the surface, if only for a moment, as we approach the subject of praying the Mass. Whatever else the Mass is, it is meant by Christ to be a prayer, in fact the most sublime prayer that a creature can make to the Creator and the one most pleasing to God.

HOW THE MASS IS A PRAYER

The Mass is a prayer because in the Eucharistic Sacrifice the faithful join with Christ in offering themselves to the heavenly Father. This is not so obvious as may seem. We are so used to thinking of prayer as saying something that we have to get hold of ourselves to recognize that prayer is also and first of all doing something.

What does Christ do? And in doing, how does He pray in the Mass? In the Mass Christ offers Himself body and soul, mind and will and emotions to His Father—even as He did at the Last Supper and as He consummated on Calvary. His original offering was not only a sacrifice, but a *complete* sacrifice, which means a holocaust. When He hung dying on the first altar of sacrifice He literally gave all that He could, because He gave all that He had as an oblation to God. If prayer is a communication between the creature and the Creator, which it is, Christ's total self-giving of His humanity to God on the cross was the most perfect communication possible. It was a conversation, indeed, but a conversation not so much in words as in deeds; in fact, in the unspeakable deed of God assuming human flesh so that as man He might surrender that flesh back to God.

Faith tells us that Christ continues doing the same in every Mass. He can no longer suffer or die because He is glorified, but He can be ready to suffer and willing to die and this readiness and willingness, we believe, is what happens the moment the two Consecrations separately take place to symbolize the separation of Christ's body and blood that brought on His death on Calvary.

However, that is not all there is to the Mass. If it were, then the Mass would be only Christ's prayer and not also ours. Whereas, it is emphatically our Mass, too, and therefore our prayer as well as His.

HOW IS THE MASS OUR PRAYER?

The Mass is our prayer insofar as we reproduce in ourselves the sentiments which animated Christ between the Last Supper and Calvary. That was a long first Mass.

What were those sentiments? They are beyond human calculation or analysis. Only in heaven shall we learn more fully what transpired in the soul and body of Christ as He was offering His body in death to His Father. But some of these sentiments have been revealed to us in the longest single revelation about the thirty-some years of Christ's mortal life. The longest part of the Gospel for a short span of time is the evangelists' minute description of almost everything that happened from the beginning of the Last Supper to Christ's final expiration on the cross. What do we find in those long Passion narratives about the sentiments which animated Christ? If we are to pray the Mass, we should duplicate in ourselves something of what went on in Him. The first Mass He offered was uniquely and exclusively His, but now it is both His Mass and ours.

During His first Mass, Christ chose—let me change the emphasis—Christ *chose* to undergo the agony, the scourging and crowning with thorns, the mockery, the way of the cross and the crucifixion. Again, during His first Mass, Christ was acting out of obedience to His heavenly Father and out of love for those whom He came to save. We seldom couple these two virtues, obedience and love, but we should. Obedience to His Father out of love for mankind. And finally, during His first Mass Christ foresaw that the sufferings He endured would last only a short time and then He would be glorified and the glory would never end. These three sets of attitudes should also be ours if we are to make of our Masses, plural—Christ's and ours now—something of what Christ made of the Mass He originally offered alone on our behalf.

1. Like Christ we are to pray that we might approximate something of His own free choice of the cross. How unnatural it seems to choose to be patient, to put up with, to be silent under rebuke, to bite one's tongue rather than speak unkindly, to hold back an angry retort, or actually smile in pardon at the one who has just offended us. No, not unnatural, but *super*natural. All of this and more is what we should expect from the Savior as we join Him in spirit in the half-million or so Masses He offers with us and for us daily throughout the Catholic world. But none of us can do this by himself. We need His help and the main source of the grace is the Mass.

2. Moreover, like Christ we ought to tell Him that whatever trials or difficulties He sends us we willingly accept in obedience to His divine will and out of love for the souls that are to be redeemed by joining our sacrifices with His. There are two divinely ordained conditions for redeeming the world; they are obedience to God and love for men. Of course, part of that obedience is to love. This means that sometimes we are called upon to love those who cause us pain. They may need the very grace that we can gain for them by our suffering *them*, and that is real love indeed.

3. Once again, like Christ, we ought to keep in mind that our life on earth, even the longest and most painful imaginable, is really very short compared with the eternity that awaits us. I used to count my years as years of twelve months each. No more. As I look back at them I count them as days. They go that fast. Everything will soon come to an end, St. Peter reminds us. Blessed Peter, thanks for saying it. So, Peter

continues, to pray better keep a calm and sober mind. "My dear people, you must not think it unaccountable that you should be tested by fire. There is nothing extraordinary in what has happened to you. If you can have some share in the sufferings of Christ, be glad, because you will enjoy a much greater gladness when His glory will be revealed." How I appreciate that future tense: "will be revealed." What strange language: "When you share in Christ's sufferings, be glad." It is not strange at all to the ears of faith, provided whatever we suffer, from a moment's inconvenience to perhaps years of estrangement, we unite the endurance twice over with Christ. We join ourselves with the Savior's passion physically, as described in the Gospels; and we join our sufferings with Him mystically, as Christ is *now* suffering in the Church, undergoing His mystical passion today. This is my favorite way of making the Way of the Cross. Fourteen stations in which Christ is *now* suffering, and we are making the *Via Crucis* with Him. What a privilege!

HOW TO PRAY THE MASS

So much for the first half of our reflections on the subject. I should like to say something more immediately practical now on how we can pray the Mass more effectively. Let me make these recommendations:

— First, understand the Mass. Whatever else the Mass is, it is a vocal prayer in which every word is vocalized and most of them aloud. Even the most reverently offered Mass takes only a short time. There is no time to be giving much immediate thought to every syllable as it comes along. Hence the wisdom of learning to understand the Mass, know it better, its mysterious meaning and profound significance through periodic reading, meditation and study beforehand. Some years ago I was asked to assemble a bibliography on the Mass for the Catholic colleges in the United States. The then-current books on the Mass in English in print were over one hundred. I wonder how many Catholics could name, I do not say ten, but even one current title on the Mass. The Mass is, indeed, a mystery. But mysteries are not only to be believed, they are with God's grace to be ever more clearly understood. We must come to better understand the Mass. A single expression like that of St. Leonard of Port Maurice can affect our whole life. "Except for the Mass," he said, "being daily offered on thousands of altars, the world would long ago have been destroyed because of its sins." I would summarize this first recommendation by using the imperative verb "meditate." *Meditate* on the Mass.

—Second, plan your Mass. If the Mass is the important action that faith tells us it is, we should plan for it. It is common knowledge and experience that we plan for things according to the importance we attach to them. Unimportant things we hardly plan for at all. Important things we plan for at length, with care. This planning can mean different things. It can mean looking ahead to know what Mass is to be said. If we wait till the Mass begins, it will take us ten minutes to find out what the Mass for today is all about. It can mean that I read the Scripture lessons beforehand, the orations, know what or whose feast is to be commemorated in the Mass. It can mean that I have given some thought before Mass to what will be said during Mass, and, I would emphasize, to what I will be thinking about during Mass. I have taught too many classes not to know, and on occasion I have had to walk into class quite unprepared. An unprepared class I might just as well have called off. It should always mean that I have a definite intention or intentions for which I will offer my Mass. Since the Mass is of infinite value, do not hesitate to multiply the intentions. I would summarize the second recommendation by saying: *anticipate* the Mass.

— Third, be attentive during Mass. The degree of participation in the new liturgy is such that most people are almost necessarily kept alert during the offering of Mass. In fact this is one of the reasons for the vernacular and the antiphonal responses between the priest or the ministers at the altar and the congregation, and the out loud saying of what used to be silent or very subdued parts of the Eucharistic rite. But the attention about which I am speaking here is something more. It is attention not only to the verbal forms being heard or said or the actions of the priest being performed, it is what I call internal attention to the mystery of faith that is being enacted before my eyes. I would compare attendance at Mass to recitation of the rosary. In both cases there are vocal prayers and silent reflection and the two should not conflict but harmonize. What I mean is that it would be well for us to mentally place ourselves — and we have many options — at the Last Supper, or the Garden of Gethsemane, or with Christ before

Herod, or before Pilate or the Sanhedrin, or on His way to Golgotha, or being nailed, or dying on the cross. Each one of us, according to our own devotion, should unite ourselves in spirit with Christ *now* as He was then in body. Let us remind ourselves that at the time when He offered His Mass, His first Mass, He had us in mind. Should we not repay Him in kind and now have *Him* in our mind in return? I would summarize this third recommendation as *concentrate.*

This past Sunday I had occasion to speak on the Holy Eucharist at the National Center of the People's Eucharistic Crusade in New York City at the Church of the Blessed Sacrament Fathers. It was inspiring to see a large church filled with fervent believers in the Holy Eucharist. What crossed my mind several times during the celebration was that all of this was due in God's Providence to the deep faith of the Founder of the Blessed Sacrament Fathers, his deep faith in the Holy Eucharist. St. Peter Julian Eymard had a vivid sense of realism as he offered Mass and he urged others to assist at Mass in the same spirit. I would like to share with you something of the easy, childlike faith of this great lover of the Eucharist, in one of his many very practical suggestions for spiritual concentration during Mass. He liked to visualize the Mass as Christ on Calvary saying His seven last words. Listen to what St. Peter Julian passed on:

"Jesus prays for His executioners: 'Father, forgive them, for they know not what they do.' Ask Jesus to forgive all your sins for you are more guilty than His executioners for having crucified Him. You sinned even though *you* knew better.

"The good thief says to Jesus: 'Lord, remember me when you come into your kingdom' and Jesus answers him: 'Amen, I say to you, this day you shall be with me in Paradise.' In his gratitude, the good thief unites his suffering with the sufferings of Jesus. Repeat his prayer in your own favor for the present moment and for the hour of *your* death.

"Jesus gives St. John to Mary for her son: 'Woman, behold your son.' John is thus to take the place of Jesus as her son and with him all mankind receives Mary for a mother. Thank our Lord for giving her to you. Ask this good mother to give you her tender love, to guide you in all things to the service of Jesus.

"'Behold your mother.' With these words, Jesus gives His mother to be our mother. Thank your loving Savior for the glorious title of child of Mary which gives you a claim to her mother's love and to all her goods and possessions.

"'I thirst.' Adore Jesus crucified anew on the altar. He prays to His heavenly Father, willing to suffer still more for the love of mankind and cries out to Him, 'I thirst.' I thirst for hearts, thirst for Your glory. Slake this burning thirst of Jesus for suffering, for the world's salvation, for reparation to the deeply offended majesty of God by suffering yourself and making reparation with Him.

"'My God, my God, why have you forsaken me?' Adore the holy and unspeakable desolation of the Savior suffered by Him to expiate your own criminal abandonment of God and His holy law. Promise Him that you will never again forsake Him.

"'It is consummated. Father, into your hands I commend my spirit.' With these words, Jesus dies. Adore Him as in this Holy Communion He delivers Himself into the hands of men, body and blood, soul and divinity—all that He is. Unite yourself with the priest and adore Jesus taken down from the cross and given into the arms of His holy mother. As you receive Him in Communion, press Him to your heart and never let Him leave you." So far St. Peter Julian. No apologies for the long quotation.

SHARE THE MASS

My last recommendation on how to pray the Mass better is to share it. What do I mean? I mean we should always remember the needs not only of ourselves but of other people while we are at Mass. There is no more effective way of drawing down God's blessing on a sinful, hungry, needy, wandering and confused world than by praying for others in the Mass and through the Mass. When St. Ignatius founded the Society of Jesus he put at the masthead of his constitutions this statement, "The most important single means by which the Society of Jesus will obtain grace from God is through the Holy Sacrifice of the Mass."

When I say, "sharing the Mass," I mean that we should share in spirit—we should join in the Masses that are being offered on so many thousands of altars throughout the Catholic Church. The Mass that we are praying is not only the Mass we are attending; it is all the Masses that Christ—the physical and mystical Christ—is offering.

What do I mean by sharing the Mass? I mean we should tell people about the Mass. To teach the Mass is to teach Christ and to teach the real Christ—the Christ who is God, who became man out of love for us and who died to prove His love. We shall be, I do not say inspired, but even reminded to tell others about the Mass and explain its meaning to them only if we ourselves have become deeply imbued with the spirit of the Mass that we have ourselves meditated upon and thoroughly understood.

By sharing the Mass, I mean we should encourage people to have Masses offered for their own and other people's intentions. This is our faith. And not just for the deceased but for the living—the living who are suffering, the living who are in need, the living who are estranged from God. There is an extraordinarily special grace for those for whom Masses are offered. We should urge people to assist at Mass in order to grow in the faith. There is no more effective way of living the Catholic Faith than by attending the Holy Sacrifice. At Mass I am not only reflecting on a revealed mystery, but I am participating in what I believe. I become part of the most important action that has ever been performed on earth—the action of God dying for man.

We should, finally, help people to profit all that they can from the Masses they assist at and from all the thousands of Masses being offered daily throughout the world. We will profit from the Mass in the exact degree that we practice the virtues that Christ lived and (I don't know how this is going to sound) *died.* Christ "died" a virtue when He offered Himself on Calvary in order that we might live, and perpetuated this cosmic event in our midst until the end of time. The Mass in which we believe is the Mass we are called upon to live. Living that Mass will mean dying the Mass. It means dying a thousand deaths to self until happily one day we shall die, like Christ, commending our spirit into the hands of the God from whom we came.

Prayer Before the Blessed Sacrament

When we speak of the Blessed Sacrament we can mean the Real Presence of Christ in the Holy Eucharist or the Holy Communion that we receive during the Eucharistic Liturgy. And the language of Catholicism does not separate the two, even while it distinguishes them. My present purpose is to look as closely as we can at one practice of Catholic piety that represents a real development of doctrine in the history of the Church, namely the practice of praying before the Blessed Sacrament, either exposed on the altar or reserved in the tabernacle. The fact of the practice is a matter of record now in the lives of many saints, even of whole religious congregations specially devoted to this custom, of the faithful in the world who have formed confraternities to make a monthly or weekly Holy Hour before the Blessed Sacrament, of the experience in the lives of thousands of priests, religious and the laity who, as by a divine instinct, are drawn to spending whatever time they can in the presence of the Real Presence of Christ in the Eucharist.

Except for saying this, it is not the focus of our reflections now. My intention is very specific — to ask, "Why?" Why should prayer before the Blessed Sacrament be specially pleasing to God, fruitful for those who pray in this way, and for those whom they pray for? Why prefer when possible this kind of prayer?"

There is more than passing value in going into this question of "Why?" For one thing there are circles and segments in the Catholic world that look with disfavor on this kind of Eucharistic prayer. I am told that in the United States the Forty Hours devotion has practically disappeared in many, perhaps most, American dioceses. I know that numerous popular devotions held in church before the Blessed Sacrament have been swept away as by a tornado. I know that in the laudable effort to highlight the Eucharistic Liturgy and therefore emphasize the altar, the tabernacle has been almost put out of sight, hidden away, as though Christ's Eucharistic Presence continuing after Mass and between Masses were something to be apologized for. I know there are speakers and writers who say things about the Real Presence which obscure the fact that Jesus Christ is really, truly and substantially present in the Blessed Sacrament not only during Mass or at Communion time but all the time, as long as the sacred elements remain. I know Pope Paul VI was so disturbed over this undercutting of the Real Presence that he did the unprecedented thing of publishing a special encyclical, *Mysterium Fidei*, right in the middle of the Second Vatican Council. Never before had this been done in the history of the ecumenical councils of the Church — that a Pope published on his own authority a universal letter to the faithful while a council was in session. He wrote it, as he said, to remind the faithful, beginning with the bishops, that the Real Presence is *real*, distinctive and absolutely unique. It is Jesus Christ abiding in our midst today.

For all of these and other painfully urgent reasons we could not spend our reflective time more profitably than to ask ourselves why every believing Catholic should make it a practice to pray as much as he can before the Blessed Sacrament on the altar. I would summarize the answer in a series of terms, with a brief commentary on each as we go along: faith in the Incarnation, faith in the Real Presence, the humanity of Christ as channel of God's power, Christ as food for the mind and will, and Christ as the object of our love.

FAITH IN THE INCARNATION

The most fundamental reason why prayer before the Blessed Sacrament is so meritorious is because it is prayer arising from faith in the cardinal mystery of Christianity, which is faith in the Incarnation. In the famous sixth chapter of John's Gospel wherein the Savior predicted the Eucharist, the whole first part of that chapter is on faith in Him as the Incarnate Son of God. Let us count the passages: first, "I am the Bread of Life. He who comes to me will never be hungry. He who believes in me will never thirst." Again, "Yes, it is my Father's will that whoever sees the Son and believes in Him shall have eternal life and that I shall raise him up on the last day." And again, "I tell you most solemnly, everybody who believes has eternal life." When, therefore, we pray before the Eucharist, whether we advert to it or not, whether we even think of it or not, we are professing in the depths of our souls our faith in Jesus Christ as the natural, only-begotten Son of the Father.

The same apostle, John, in his first letter comes back to the same theme, only this time in the strongest words ever spoken by man on what is the foundation stone of the Christian religion. Says John, "Whoever believes that Jesus is the Christ has been begotten by God." Then the promise written under divine inspiration, "Who can overcome the world? Only the man who believes that Jesus is the Son of God." Everyone else will be overcome by the world.

So the first reason why prayer before the Blessed Sacrament is so important is because it is an expression of faith in the divinity of Christ, that is, in the Son of Mary who is the Son of God, who is here, right here and now before me, as close and perhaps closer than were the people on the hillside near the Sea of Galilee when Jesus first predicted the Holy Eucharist.

FAITH IN THE REAL PRESENCE

Another reason why prayer before the Blessed Sacrament is so praiseworthy is because it is a profession of faith in the real bodily presence of Jesus under the sacramental veils. On the same occasion when the Savior foretold the Eucharist He so intertwined two objects of faith as to make them almost inseparable. Let me change it — so closely did He intertwine them that for all time they remain inseparable: faith in His divinity and faith in His Eucharistic humanity, otherwise known as the Real Presence. Recall what happened after hearing what He said. Many of His followers said to themselves, "This is intolerable language. How could anyone accept it?" After this we are further told "many" — note — "many of his disciples," not merely the onlookers or the crowd, but "many of his disciples left him and stopped going with him." Everyone who prays before the Blessed Sacrament is in effect choosing to not only go along with Christ, but physically comes to Christ. Why? Because he believes. Believes what? Believes that behind the external appearances of bread is a Man and behind the Man is God. He or she believes that the Christ who is in the church or chapel is the same who was conceived at Nazareth, who was born at Bethlehem, who fled into Egypt, who lived for thirty years in the same town in which He was conceived, who preached and worked miracles throughout Palestine, who died on the cross on Calvary, rose from the dead and ascended to His Father at Jerusalem. The same Jesus who was there in a definite geographic locality is now here also in a definite geographic place in whatever city or town where the Blessed Sacrament is reserved. This is the Christ of history and the Christ — how I like to say it — of geography.

If, as the apostle tells us, without faith no one can please God, so without faith no one can hope to obtain anything from God. On both counts the believer who prays before the Eucharist is a believer indeed. He believes that Jesus Christ is the man from Nazareth, but that this man is the eternal God. He further believes that this same Jesus who is God made man is present as man on earth today: that He is only feet away from me when I pray before Him; that in the Eucharist He has the same human body and soul, hands and feet, and Sacred Heart as He has now in heaven, as He had during His visible stay in the area we now call the Near East. The pray-er before the Eucharist believes that time is erased by the miracle of the Real Presence and so is distance and space. He believes that what Martha told Mary on the occasion of Christ's visit is being told to him or her: "The Master is here and He wants to see you." Hearing this, we are informed, Mary got up quickly and went to Him. That is what every worshipper before the Eucharist does: gets up quickly from wherever he or she may be and goes to the Master who is here waiting for us.

THE HUMANITY OF CHRIST AS A CHANNEL OF GRACE

Once we establish the fact of faith that the same Jesus is in the Eucharist as was on earth in New Testament times, it is not difficult to appreciate the third reason why prayer before the Blessed Sacrament is so efficacious. As we read the pages of the Gospels we are struck by the marvelous power that Christ's humanity had in effecting changes in the persons who came into contact with Him. For

the sake of convenience we limit ourselves to
two short episodes from the Gospel according
to St. Mark.

First episode: when the disciples with
Christ were in the boat at sea and a terrible storm
broke out, Jesus, who was asleep, got up and re-
buked the wind and said to the seas, "Quiet now,
be calm!" And the wind dropped and all was
calm again. This was the Creator of the wind and
the Maker of the seas commanding His creatures.
No wonder they obeyed! But He spoke with human lips and pronounced human words as man.

Second episode: when the woman with the
hemorrhage who had been ill for a dozen years
came up behind Jesus, she said to herself, "If
I can even touch His clothes I shall be well
again." She touched His clothes and was in-
stantly healed. Mark makes a significant observation about Jesus: "Immediately," he says,
"Christ was aware that power had gone out from
Him. He turned around in the crowd and asked,
'Who touched my clothes?'" When the frightened woman admitted what she had done, the
Savior praised her, "My daughter, your faith has
restored you to health."

All through the Gospels during His public
life, the humanity of Christ was the instrument
of great power that went out from Him to work
signs and wonders such as the world had never
seen. These signs and wonders were performed
by divine power, of course, but through the humanity of Jesus Christ. Healing lepers and the
blind, driving out demons, restoring strength
to those who were maimed or paralyzed, even
raising the dead back to life—always it was the
human nature through which the God-man mani-
fested His power and conferred blessings on a

suffering and sinful mankind. What He did then, He wants to continue till the end of time. All grace, all power, all blessing comes from God; but all grace, all power and all blessing comes — we believe, uniquely (this is our faith) — comes uniquely through the humanity of the Son of God. This humanity, as we know, operates in many ways, but it acts nowhere more effectively — and I wish to add, miraculously — than through the human nature that is substantially united to the divinity in the Blessed Sacrament.

As then, so now, the power is there, the potential miracles are there, but no less than during His visible stay on earth — and He is on earth, honest; He really is — the condition was faith. The condition *is* faith. What Christ requires of those in whose favor He wants now, as then, to work the signs and wonders that will draw bodies and souls to Himself is faith.

CHRIST AS FOOD FOR THE MIND AND WILL

One of the best ways to look at prayer before the Blessed Sacrament is to see it as an extension of Holy Communion. Christ Himself could not have been plainer when He called Himself "the Bread of Life" and told us to eat His Body and drink His Blood. What we may overlook, however, is that the spiritual nourishment that comes from the Eucharist does not end with Holy Communion. Of course, there is an efficacy that comes from the actual reception of the Sacrament that is special and distinctive, but we are not talking about that now. There is also a nourishment that takes place in what we may casually call "spiritual communion." How cheap the phrase sounds! But it is neither casual nor cheap. It is profoundly meaningful. As we pray before the Blessed Sacrament our souls are fed by the Person of the Savior in the two faculties of spirit that need to be constantly fed. They are the mind and the will. In the mind we need light; in the will we need strength. And both needs are met in an extraordinary way through earnest prayer before the Eucharist. Remember we said it is still the Blessed Sacrament. It is not the residue of the Sacrament. It is not the remnants after the Sacrament. It is not a memory of the Blessed Sacrament. It *is* the Blessed Sacrament.

We might ask: why not? Is it not the same Christ who taught the multitudes, who gave the sermon on the mount and who took time, and a lot of time, to tell His disciples and to further share with them the secrets that until then had been hidden from the minds of men? It is Jesus and He is here. We would not expect His lips to be sealed. He has a message to give and we have a lot to learn. Did He not say He was the Truth and the Way—the Truth who knows what we should know and the Way who knows how we should serve almighty God? It is this Truth and Way become Incarnate who is with us and near and available to us. All we need to do is to believe sufficiently, to come to Him in the Blessed Sacrament and ask very simply, "Lord, teach me. I'm dumb." And that is no exaggeration! "Your servant is listening and ready to learn."

In the will we need strength to supply for the notorious weakness that by now we are almost ashamed to call our own. How well it is that other people do not know how really stupid and weak we are. What a precious secret! But again, is it not the same Christ who encouraged the disciples, who braced up the faltering Peter and promised to be with us all days? That promise is to be taken literally. He is here. Jesus is here telling us today, "Peace I bequeath to you. My own peace I give you." Thanks, Lord, I sure need it!

"Do not let your hearts be troubled or afraid." How well you know, Lord, I'm scared. "Have courage; I have overcome the world." No less than then, so now Christ is not merely encouraging us in words, which we appreciate, but strengthening us with grace. His words, being those of God, are grace. And the words and the grace are once more accessible to all who come to Him as He foretold, "Come to me all you who labor and are overburdened and I will give you strength." Jesus, that is me. But we must come to Him, the Emmanuel, in the Eucharist to tell Him what we need. If we do and as often as we do He will do the rest.

CHRIST THE OBJECT OF OUR LOVE

The final and in a way most important reason why prayer before the Blessed Sacrament is so important is that when we pray before the Eucharist we have before us in human form the principal reason for our existence, which is the all-loving God. Already in Deuteronomy in the Old Testament the Jews were told, "Listen, Israel, Yahweh, our God, is the one Yahweh. You shall love your God with all your heart, with all your soul, with all your strength." But, what a difference between the Old and the New Testaments: what God did in the meantime, and that is what made the New Testament *new* — He became Man. He became Incarnate, which means God became Man and as man He gave us the Eucharist which is the Real Presence. Why? We have seen other reasons; this is the main one: mainly to show us how much He loves us by being with us in order that we might be with Him. There was never a more important prepositional phrase in human language: to be with Him, to tell Him how much we love Him in return.

St. Margaret Mary was chosen by Providence, as Christ told her, principally to restore to a loveless world the practice of the love of God. What was the principal means that she was to tell the faithful to use to restore this neglected love? It was devotion to the Blessed Sacrament where, as the Savior complained, in the greatest manifestation of His love He is most neglected and forgotten, and worst of all by souls who are consecrated to Him by the sacred bonds of the priesthood and religious life. I cannot think of anything that the Catholic Church, especially in our day, needs more than thousands of souls in every walk of life who pray daily before the Blessed Sacrament, telling God who is there in the flesh in the Eucharist how much they love Him and asking Him for the most important favor we can ask of God: to love Him still more.

I would like to close with a prayer composed by St. Margaret Mary's confessor and counselor, Blessed Claude Colombiere, in which he expressed the kind of sentiments of love that we should express in our own words as we pray before the Blessed Sacrament where Christ our God in human form is near us. Prayed Blessed Claude: "To make reparation for so many outrages and such cruel ingratitude, most adorable and lovable Heart of my lovable Jesus, and to avoid falling as far as it is in my power to do so into a like misfortune, I offer You my heart with all the movements of which it is capable. I give myself entirely to You, and from this hour I protest most sincerely that I desire to forget myself and all that have any connection with me. I wish to remove the obstacle which could prevent my entering into this divine Heart which You have had the goodness to open to me and into which I desire to enter, there to live and to die with Your faithful servants entirely penetrated and enflamed with Your love."

These sentiments can be our own, believing as we do that the Jesus to whom we are thus speaking is a man like us, but also our God. "I love those who love me; those who seek me eagerly shall find me," was the prophecy foretold by Wisdom in the Old Law. It is fulfilled in the New Law for those who believe literally in the Real Presence and act on what they believe.

Spiritual Reading— Who Needs It?

I am afraid that for many Catholics the term "spiritual reading" is either a strange expression, and they are not sure what it means, or they have heard that monks and nuns do it—whatever it is. But spiritual reading is neither strange nor exotic as by now centuries of Christian experience testifies. In order to do some justice to this very practical subject I propose to ask a series of questions and answer them as we go along. My hope is to end up with one good answer to the one question which is the subject of our reflections: spiritual reading —who needs it?

Why is reading, any reading, important? Why is reading influential? What is spiritual reading? Why is spiritual reading necessary? Then a few closing words about implications.

WHY READING IS IMPORTANT

We begin to get some idea about the importance of reading from the simple fact that so many people are doing it. Thousands of newspapers throughout the world, some with daily circulations of more than a million; thousands of periodicals, some with monthly circulations of many millions; thousands of books published annually, some by now with a publication history that is astronomical. Reading must be important seeing the influence that the printed word has had on human civilization.

A good date for dating the beginning of the modern world is the dawn of the age of print. Man's history will never be the same. But the real proof for the significance of the printed word is the seldom realized fact that when God began what we call His public revelation, first to the Jews and then to the people of the New Israel who followed Christ, He made sure that the substance of this revelation was not only communicated orally, but was written down under divine inspiration. The existence of the Bible, written in an age when very few people could read or write, is a lasting testimonial to what the Holy Spirit thinks of reading. He first of all made sure that the Semitic people discovered what we call phonetic writing about 2,000 B.C. and then provided to inspire persons to set down on parchment what God wanted all mankind to know about the divine mind and will until the end of time. God invented writing to make the reading of Scriptures possible.

WHY IS READING INFLUENTIAL?

Not only is reading important, but perhaps more than any other means of social communication it is in my judgment the most influential. This calls for some explanation in view of the marvelous discoveries of the electronics media—the telephone and telegraph, radio and television, the film and radar and their derivatives. I have no intention of making any competitive comparisons between the written word and other means of transmitting ideas or attitudes from one person to others. My intention is the more practical one of emphasizing why the written, generally the printed word, is so influential.

Reading is so influential because the ideas expressed in a piece of good writing are concentrated, they are not diffused. Again, what is published is, by the law of economics if for no other reason, done professionally by persons who know what they are saying and say it intelligently and persuasively, even when they may not be writing truthfully. The written word, being in competition with other written words, is done carefully and by and large in such a way that a maximum of thought goes into a minimum of content. Moreover, what is being read is normally done in solitude—the mind of the writer affecting the mind of the reader in a quiet, reflective and by definition sympathetic mood. If I don't like what I'm reading I simply close the book and the author never knows. Whereas when I am speaking I know exactly when somebody in the audience does not want to listen. If they are kind they go to sleep. Some manifest their being bored or displeased in more dramatic ways. But not so with readers. The one who reads wants to be told. Still again, what is read remains written. Whence for all times has remained as part of our faith the famous words of Pilate: "Quod scripsi scripsi" (What I have written, is written.) Consequently it can be read and reread years, centuries later. What is written, as every author hopes, is written not only for his own generation but for generations yet unborn.

Finally, unlike in other forms of discourse, the written word can be gone over and analyzed. It can be studied and scrutinized and as a consequence it can have an impact on the human spirit that is incalculable. It is therefore understandably indelible. Somewhere years ago when I began studying Latin there was a phrase written which you may be sure I memorized: "Verba volant, scripta manent. Spoken words fly, what is written stays."

WHAT IS SPIRITUAL READING?

We can begin by describing it in terms of what it is not and that is easy. Spiritual reading is not secular reading. But more positively spiritual reading is that reading whose purpose as writing is to assist the believer to better know, love, and serve God and thereby become more God-like, which means more holy, especially in his life of prayer and the practice of Christian virtue. Notice I said that spiritual reading is that reading whose purpose as *writing* is to assist the believer. Why put it just that way? Sounds odd! The reason is that there is a sense in which any kind of reading, even the most obviously secular, like the daily papers or a popular novel, may, and by now I have been told, is considered spiritual reading when my purpose in reading is spiritual. By that standard, reading *Time* or *Newsweek* or worse, provided a person could say "my purpose is spiritual," makes it spiritual. Not so. You cannot canonize the secular.

I am not here then speaking of spiritual reading in that broad sense. Spiritual reading in our consideration is writing that was written with a spiritual purpose and not only one that may happen to be read with perhaps a religious intention in mind. Quite frankly, all our reading —even the most secular—should be spiritualized, but that is not the same as spiritual reading.

Concretely the forms that this kind of spiritual reading can take are not as numerous as may seem. I will reduce them to five—just five: the Scriptures or the Bible; the teachings of the Church or Sacred Doctrine; the History of the Church in general or any one of the myriad of aspects of the Church's passage through time; biography or the lives and thoughts of saintly persons, either by themselves or by someone else; then, in a class by itself, any kind of reflection on any of the preceding categories which may be learned or personal, scholarly or practical, or any combination of these. You will notice where I placed the last category, in the last place.

WHY IS SPIRITUAL READING NECESSARY?

Spiritual reading is necessary as the normal way of nourishing the Christian faith, which means getting food for the mind so that the will and affections might love and serve God accordingly. I say the normal way, allowing for exceptions that simply prove the rule. We must take the ordinary means to preserve our physical life and the obligation is a grave one. Among these ordinary means none is more basic than food for the body. Without eating the body dies. And it is no comfort to say I am alive now and there is food outside of me. Either that good gets inside of me or I die. Being near me is not enough. I can be surrounded by food and starve. So too we must take the ordinary means to preserve our supernatural life and again the obligation is a grave one. Among these ordinary means none is more basic than food for the mind to nourish the faith. Without food for the mind the faith withers and dies, and there is no mental nourishment for the soul more available and accessible and providable than spiritual reading as just described. Not to nourish the mind, and in the mind the faith, with this food is to tempt Providence, which means to tempt God.

Pause for a moment to reflect on the millions of thought hours spent daily in a single large American city literally devouring the pabulum dished out in such truckloads to the people. Then ask yourself how many of these people spend one tenth of one percent of their mind-life a day reading, say, the inspired text of the

Bible or the documents of the Church or the life of a saint, and you begin to see how urgently necessary it is to convince ourselves and those under our care that they *must* do spiritual reading. Otherwise, they will spiritually die, and they are dying.

If we further reflect on the other millions of, shall I call them thought hours, that people spend watching television or listening to the radio, the urgency of what we are saying becomes even more imperative. There *must* be, *absolutely must be* a steady diet of sound nourishment for the soul at the risk of losing one's spiritual life, and that is the verdict of Christian history. However, this necessity is not only for survival, it is also and especially for spiritual growth. If I wish to have God on my mind during the day, I must read about God and what He has to say. That is why He spoke. It would in effect be telling God: "Well, I've heard that, come to think of it, there are some writings they tell me You inspired. How interesting!" And then not even pay God the courtesy of reading what He said.

If I wish to talk to God in humble and easy conversation I must read about what God is, what He has done, and is doing in ages past and today, so that I might have something to talk about when I am in prayer. As we know now from experience the surest way of lapsing into silence is to enter a person's company having nothing on my mind to say. If I wish to develop a strong Catholic faith that is clear and sound and un-alloyed, I must read what the Catholic Church teaches, since her teaching comes to me espe-cially in written form. But let me make sure I read what the Catholic Church teaches. If I read, which I should, what others tell me about what she teaches or explain to me either God's revelation or the Church's doctrine, let me again make sure they are persons who themselves are faithful to the Church, and who love the Church. Not everyone who writes about the Church loves her.

Moreover, if I wish to make sense of what is happening in the Church today I must read about what happened in the Church yesterday. If I am to be inspired by the Mystical Body of Christ, I must know this is not only the post-conciliar territory in which I live; it is not only that short span of time which I call today. The Mystical Body has a history. It has had centuries of suffering and persecution. It has struggled and fought with error, and has marvelously, not only survived, but thrived on opposition. If I am to be strong in my faith in this century, I'd better know something about what the faith of believers before me taught them. Otherwise, as so many are doing today, we are liable to barter our faith for a mess of pottage. All of this means I must read the history of the Mystical Body and identify myself in spirit with the by now millions who have believed before me, with the hundreds of thousands who shed their blood in defense of the faith that I treasure. I will thus be inspired to do my share in preserving and extending and nourishing the faith by laboring in the Church's apostolate.

If I wish to become holy I must read about holy people. Their faith will strengthen mine. Their trust in divine providence will encourage mine. Above all their victory over self, the world and the evil spirit will spur me on to victory. How we need this encouragement! Only saints reproduce saints.

There is such a thing as supernatural genealogy. Unless I read the lives of saintly people, their sentiments, their trials and victories, how can they reproduce themselves in me?

I still have a few simple implications. By now one implication should be clear enough: Who needs spiritual reading? *Everyone who wants to become Christlike!* There is no choice. The Savior is not for nothing called the Word of God. We seldom think of Him as also—how I like the phrase—the Written Word of God, written in the Gospels which describe His life and in the apostolic writings His life inspired; written in the Church He founded and of which He continues as her invisible Head; written in the saintly men and women who are faithful images of what their Master had been. This Master is unique. He not only teaches, He reproduces. All of this is ready to be read by us, if only we are willing to read. Christ, we are told by St. John, is the light that shines in the dark. And, if we are honest, we must admit how dark the darkness is. We need Him, the Light of our own world, to enlighten us about how we are to serve Him, so that we might love Him and bring others to love and serve Him too.

Achieving
Peace of Mind

There is hardly much need telling ourselves or proving to others that ours is a restless age. Instability and insecurity are everywhere. There is uncertainty among the young who are worried about their future. There is uncertainty among parents who are concerned about their children. There is uncertainty among workers who are unsure of their jobs. There is uncertainty, it seems, at every age and social level and in almost every walk of life. Yet this is more a background to what I really wish to say which is how to cope with insecurity not only among people but within people, in a word, how does a person remain constant in a world of inconstancy and change?

We get some idea of the gravity of the situation once we realize that millions of Americans must be unhappy as seen in their preoccupation with sex, drugs and drink. They maintain some semblance of security by escaping from the realities of life into a world of fantasy created by the media and sustained by the advertising industry. As a Christian believer looks at all of this he asks himself, "Is this the way it should be? Or is there something wrong? And what can I do to achieve and maintain my own peace of mind?" The answer is *yes*. There is something radically wrong and there is plenty that I can do to be at peace and help others become peaceful too.

TWO KINDS OF PEACE OF SOUL

Nothing should be clearer to a person who believes in Christ and the Church than that we are meant to be at peace not only between ourselves, which is external, but within ourselves, which is deeply interior. Shalom, the Hebrew word for peace, was built into all the messianic prophecies. And Jerusalem, the City of Peace, was the symbol of what the messianic kingdom was to be. Peace was the theme of the angels' song at Bethlehem. It was the theme of Christ's promise to His followers the night before He died. It was His first message to the apostles the day He rose from the dead. In the Eucharistic liturgy how often the Church has us pray for peace. And how earnestly we hope to obtain peace if we lack it, or retain it if we already have what must surely be counted man's single greatest possession on earth this side of the vision of God: to be at peace.

Interior peace is of two kinds: one in the heart or will and the other in the mind or intellect. They are closely connected but they are not the same. Peace of heart for the believing Christian is the absence of conflict between his will and that of others and ultimately between his will and the will of God. My heart is at peace when I want what God wants, when I desire only what He desires. It is in this sense that the inspired writer asks and does not have to answer his own question addressed to God, "Who has ever resisted Your will, O Lord, and been at peace?" There was no need for a reply. The answer is *no one.*

Peace of mind, on the other hand, for the believing Christian is the absence of conflict between his mind and the mind of others and ultimately between his mind and the infinite mind of God. My mind is at peace when I know what God knows insofar as a creature can participate in the ocean of divine wisdom. My mind is at peace when I assent because I want to do whatever God has revealed. Not because I understand what this means or can explain the mysteries of revelation, but because I trust in God's authority and submit my intellect to His. In a word, I have peace of mind when I have the truth; when my thoughts agree with God's thoughts, and my judgments correspond to His I have the truth and I am at peace. Peace of mind, then, is the experience of the truth. It is the result of truth. It is the fruit of truth. I shall have only as much peace of mind as I am in possession of the truth, especially of that truth which God has revealed and bids us to believe.

How, we now ask, are the two forms of peace – of heart and of mind – related? They are related as cause and effect, where peace of mind is the cause and the condition for peace of heart. How can anyone want what God wants unless he first knows what God wants him to know and therefore should desire? God wants me to love Him, but I must first know Him. God wants me to love others as I love myself, but I must know that first. God wants me to be humble and prayerful and chaste, but I must first know that He wants humility and prayer and chastity and know also the means He has given me to grow in these virtues before I can efficaciously desire them or even less experience the peace that their faithful practice infallibly brings.

What are we saying? We are saying that if we wish to have peace of heart, which means tranquility of spirit in our affections, we must first have the truth in our minds. Otherwise we are pursuing shadows and running after the wind. Suppose I do not know because I do not believe that my first duty as a Christian is to seek the kingdom of God and His justice. I just do not know that because I do not believe it. And all belief is fundamentally in the mind. Suppose I do not know because I do not believe that provided I seek God and His kingdom first all other things will be added unto me. Suppose I think the opposite, that I am to place creatures first and seek God—if I seek Him at all—last. That is untrue, but suppose I do not know, or worse, suppose I really think that what is a lie is the truth and I act on the lie. Can I on these premises have peace of heart? Absolutely not— as by now myriads of human beings are finding out to their disillusionment and often to their despair. Truth in the mind, therefore, is peace of mind, and peace of mind is indispensable for peace of heart.

No doubt God is merciful in dealing with His sometimes not-so-rational creatures. In His goodness He often makes up for what we lack. In His mercy He may give more peace to a person who through no fault of his own knows less revealed truth than to another, say, who knows more. But having said that, God cannot contradict Himself. The truth, He told us, will make us free. Free from what? Free from fear. Free from insecurity. Free from worry. Free from anxiety. Of course, I must not only have the truth, but use it. I must act on what faith tells me is the truth and the peace that Christ promised will be mine.

HOW TO ACHIEVE PEACE OF MIND

If peace of mind means the possession of God's truth, it naturally follows that everything depends on our having this truth and all we have to do is use the means required for getting the truth. At this point I wish to briefly state and then explain how to go about getting the truth, which is another way of saying how to go about attaining peace of mind. I would capsulize my recommendations in these words: seek and protect and live the truth, and peace of mind is attained.

Seek the truth. It may strike us as a bit odd for Christ to more than once insist on His followers searching for what evidently God wants to give us. Is this a game? He tells us to search and seek and look for and only if we do the searching or seeking shall we find; and He gave us a whole parable on the woman looking for the lost coin. The point is that if we are to come into the possession of the truth that God has revealed we must go out to find it. The truth forces itself on no one's mind. This means a variety of things. It most obviously means that I must go out of my own laziness and complacency and exercise at least my instinct of curiosity to learn what God has taught mankind, with at least as much eagerness as worldly people show in their insatiable hunger for secular knowledge. Our universities are bulging with millions of students hungering for knowledge and information. About what? About how to make a better living or make more money or just to satisfy the natural craving to better understand the universe of space and time and people and events of past and present history. But by comparison how few are all that interested in learning about God and His dealings with man.

It is not enough however only to wish to find the truth and to take the trouble of learning. We must also know where it is to be found. It is not so easy, not as easy as it seems, nor even as easy as it used to be. Time was when you could look at the cover of a book and read the book with security that you were getting the truth. But in case you have not heard, no more. I am speaking of religious truth and specifically of revealed truth. Too many once trustworthy sources of religious truth have either become dried up or so polluted that sometimes it makes a Catholic feel like the Greek Diogenes who went in search of an honest man with a lamp and he would cry out if he found one, "Eureka!"

Let me suggest three simple norms for discovering religious truth in today's miasma of very sophisticated and very learned confusion. Ask yourself three questions. Question one: does what I am hearing or reading correspond to what the Church has always held to be true? If it does you can trust it. If it does not, distrust it. The Church has always held that Christ is bodily present in the Eucharist; that the Pope is infallible in teaching the universal Church; that marriage is indissoluble by any human authority, civil or ecclesiastical; that adultery and fornication and homosexuality are mortal sins that deprive those who die thus estranged from God of the vision of God; that the priesthood is reserved for men; that personal auricular confession is necessary to obtain sacramental absolution; that the Mass is a sacrifice and not just an elaborate liturgical meal; that direct abortion is murder; that obedience to rightful authority is a divine law; that religious life is part of divine revelation; that celibacy is pleasing to God; that contraception, no matter what the intention, is a grave sin; that prayer is necessary for salvation; and that angels are sent by God to minister to our human and especially our spiritual needs. All of these, and I could go on, are truths the Church has always held. Anyone who contradicts or casts doubt on what has been the heritage of historic Christianity, no matter how articulate or learned or highly placed he or she may be, is not telling the truth.

Second question: does what I am hearing or reading conform to the present teaching of the Roman Catholic Church as expressed by the

Vicar of Christ? If it does you can trust it. If it does not, distrust it no matter how otherwise pious or scholarly the opinion or theory may be. That is all it is, an opinion or theory, and it should be treated accordingly.

Third question: what kind of a person, morally, is the one who is teaching or writing what I hear or read? We did not used to have to ask these questions. We do now. Is he or she humble and prayerful and charitable and patient and chaste, or the opposite? More than once the Savior used this norm and He wants us to use it too to explain why His critics who finally crucified Him, the scribes and pharisees, were not teaching the truth. Their pride and envy, among other vices, as He said, disqualified them from being taken seriously.

One more question, a kind of addendum, but it should also be asked, "What are the consequences of the ideas I am reading or hearing?" Again the Savior is our Master in applying this precious norm when He tells us that by their fruits you shall know them. Ideas have consequences. True ideas have good consequences. False ideas have bad consequences. There is no escaping the logic of this divinely ordained law of spiritual fertility: truth always begets goodness, falsehood always begets evil.

A good checklist of the procreative power of truth and the corresponding power of falsehood to beget evil is given by St. Paul in his letter to the Galatians. His study in contrast between the progeny of error and truth is worth quoting in full. What is the offspring of error?

It is "fornication, gross indecency and sexual irresponsibility, idolatry and sorcery; feuds and wrangling, jealousy, bad temper and quarrels; disagreements, factions, envy; drunkenness, orgies and similar things." What is the offspring of truth? It is the very opposite: "love, joy, peace, patience, kindness, goodness, trustfulness, gentleness and self-control." Here we have a divinely revealed, and easily applied rule for the discernment of spirits. If the untruth is active, the moral effects of false ideas are invariably bad. If the Spirit of truth is at work, the moral results are correspondingly, and infallibly, good.

Protect the truth. Discovering God's truth, however, and acquiring it is only the beginning. We must also preserve it. Otherwise the peace that depends on the possession of truth may be lost. If we are not only to achieve peace of mind but retain it, we must protect the truth we already have. Otherwise, as Christ explained in the parable of the seed, the enemy of human nature will steal it away.

Let us listen for a moment to the context in which the Savior gave the parable. He was talking about a man going out to sow his seed, but the seed fell on different kinds of ground and the results were predictable. For our purpose, only the first of the four kinds of ground concerns us here. The seeds, which Christ said are the Word of God's truth, falling on the edge of the path, did not produce fruit. Why? Because the birds came and ate them up. When Christ later explained the meaning to the disciples, He said, "When anyone hears the Word of the kingdom without understanding, the evil one comes and carries off what was sown in his heart."

The lesson should be clear. In order to protect the truth of God's Word in our mind we must as far as humanly possible make it our own, appropriate it, assimilate it, in a word, we must come to understand what we believe. And there is no more assured way of obtaining this necessary understanding of God's truth than by meditating on it. This is a one word reason, the fundamental reason, for meditation: to understand God's truth. Everything else depends on that. Christ said so. Daily reflection on the mysteries of faith is indispensable to keep the faith, which means to keep the truth. There is no substitute. Such meditation will preserve the believer from the tragedy that has befallen so many once-believing Catholics, including not a few priests and religious. Let us never suppose the devil is not interested in those who believe revealed truth. He is so interested that he uses his shrewdest strategy to dislodge the faith-security of the firmest believers. Be sure of this: the more firmly you believe, the more strongly the devil is trying to steal away the seed of God's Word sown in your mind.

Recall the first time the devil appears in the pages of Sacred Scripture right after the creation of the world and the creation of Adam and Eve. Recall what the devil did. How did he get our first parents to fall? He began by tempting Eve, who in turn was supposed to tempt Adam. The devil's first recorded words are a question: "Did God really say you are not to eat from any of the trees in the garden?" Notice the demonic technique. He raised a question in order to raise a doubt in the mind of Eve and the rest is a matter of salvation history.

In order to protect the truth we believe, we must look at this truth in God's presence, think about it, relish it, in a word, come to love it through frequent prayerful meditation. Otherwise we run the risk of having the devil raise doubts in our minds and once we begin to doubt we are likely to end denying even the most fundamental truths of our faith. This is not my recommendation—it is not even just a recommendation—it is a requirement taught by Christ as a condition for remaining true to the truth that He became man to reveal, that is, to sow in our minds.

Live the truth. Finding the truth and even preserving it by prayerful reading, study and reflection are not enough. We are also to practice the truth. Achieving peace is a state of spiritual perfection in which every Christian believer should grow and with God's grace improve as he goes through life.

We must, therefore, live the truth we believe if we are to expect to acquire the kind of peace that God has in store for those who believe in His name. The whole thing is beautifully outlined by Jesus in His sermon at the Last Supper. He tells us, "If you keep my commandments you will remain in my love. I have told you this that my joy may be in you and your joy be complete." What is Christ telling us? He is telling us not only to believe what He reveals, but to do it. Not only to assent with our minds, but practice it in our lives. Let us make sure we know what He means. What He means is that the truths of revelation are mysteries indeed that are to be accepted on faith and believed in without fully being understood. But they are not mental puzzles, or riddles, as it were. They are demands on our will. That is why Christ calls them "commandments."

We seldom identify two words — mystery and commandment — but notice what follows. Provided we submit our wills to divine truth and act on what we believe, something wonderful happens in our lives — we attain not only peace of soul, but spiritual joy as our reward already in this life and long before eternity. This joy, the kind that Christ calls "my joy," He shares with no one except the person who lives out the truth that He, Incarnate Truth, had revealed. The degree of this joy and its depth are in proportion to our generosity in doing what we think, that is, in being what we subscribe to on faith. No wonder the saints were such happy persons whose assimilation to Christ crucified was ironically so great. They learned what all of us should know: that we have fully achieved peace of mind, which is deep interior joy, when we behave as we believe. This means that we have come to share in the cross of Jesus Christ.

How To Live in the Presence of God

As we reread the New Testament, we may be struck by the insistence on certain practices that, until we take a second look, we might take for granted. One such teaching, that I would call the single, most effective way of living our Christian faith, is the practice of the presence of God. My intention is to quote in sequence the classic passages in the New Testament where this practice is urged on the faithful. With each passage I shall explain what it means, while applying what the Holy Spirit is telling us to our own daily lives.

PRAY CONTINUALLY

The first occasion we meet this injunction is in the Gospel of St. Luke when the Savior is described by the evangelist as telling His followers about the need to pray continually and never to lose heart. Let us think seriously about what we are told. We need, that is we should, or better we must pray continually. It is a universal duty that applies to all believers. It is meant not only for priests or religious, but for everyone who professes to believe in the Gospels and claims to be a follower of Jesus Christ. To leave no doubt about the obligation, we are further told to pray so constantly as never to lose heart. This means that we are both commanded to pray always and then, if you please, forbidden to cease doing so.

What can the Holy Spirit possibly mean? He cannot mean for us to be always engaged in vocal prayer. That is out of the question. Nor even always in mental prayer. That too is impossible. What kind of prayer are we bidden to practice without ceasing? It is the prayer of the heart. It is the kind that St. Paul also tells Christians to practice when he bids them: "Pray constantly."

What kind of prayer is prayer of the heart? It is the immediate effect of divine grace, whereby a person in God's friendship is disposed to do the will of God. It need not be actual prayer, which is our love of God put into conscious practice. It is rather habitual prayer, that we may define as the disposition or readiness for the practice of our love of God. Spiritual masters explain how easy and spontaneous this kind of prayer should be. Why? Because for a person in grace it is as natural to pray always as it is to love always. A person can love God always without always thinking of God or telling Him of one's love. It is enough if we are determined not only to do nothing contrary to the will of God at any time, but also take every available opportunity to prove our love and make acts of love whenever grace prompts us to do so. It must be in this way that a mother loves her children, a wife her husband, and a friend loves a friend. The person whom one loves may not have been on the mind, but the moment the person comes to mind, immediately a feeling of affection is aroused.

People in love would gladly keep the beloved image always present, and if the mind is devoted to other objects because it has to, the heart never is. It is the same with prayer. We are said to pray always when we wish to, if it were possible, when we never lose an opportunity to pray, but especially if we are always ready to cooperate with the inspirations of grace.

DO EVERYTHING IN THE NAME OF THE LORD JESUS

Properly understood, this attitude of soul, that we call prayer of the heart, is not hindered by the numerous occupations and responsibilities of daily life. Quite the contrary. These duties are precisely God's way of providing us with opportunities for putting our prayer of the heart into practice. On this level there are no distractions in prayer, because what we might call distractions are ways in which this prayer of heart is exercised. St. Paul again could not have been plainer. "Never say or do anything," he tells us, "except in the name of the Lord Jesus." Then he goes on to enumerate a dozen and more examples of how this is to be done.

Wives are to give way to their husbands. Husbands are to love their wives and treat them with gentleness. Children are to be obedient to their parents. Parents are not to drive their children to resentment. Servants are to be obedient to their masters. Masters are to treat their servants with justice and fairness. Christians are to be tactful in dealing with those who are not Christians. So the Pauline explanation goes on as to what it means to do everything in the name of the Lord Jesus. Paul means everything.

Elsewhere the Apostle is more sweeping in his declaration. "Whatever you eat, whatever you drink, whatever you do, do it all for the glory of God." The reference to eating and drinking may seem to be trivial. But it is not trivial at all. What the emphasis is, is that nothing is exempted or excepted from the ambit of doing it for God's glory, and therefore according to His will. This is not child's play, as by now a lifetime of experience must have taught us. Of course, we eat, and we drink and we do a lot of things. That is not what Paul is saying. We are to do all these things for the glory of God. Although it is not child's play, it is something that even a child can understand. Meaning what? Meaning that I am ready and willing at every moment, in every situation, to do what God wants me to do. This may be being patient with a person who naturally bores me. And I don't show that I am bored. Being kind to a person who has never shown, as far as my memory can recall, any kindness to me. Being prompt in rising out of bed. Prompt for my work. Prompt in keeping appointments. Prompt in answering letters and paying my bills. Being forebearing with the slow when I am early, and not being upset with those who show up early when I am late. Being communicative in conversation with people who want me to speak, and silent when it is wiser to hold my tongue. This doing everything, and it is everything, for the glory of God implies three things: first, that I take the trouble to find out what God wants; second, that I take time out to learn how He wants me to do it; and third, that I do it.

It is remarkable how many otherwise good people proceed through steps one and two, but so often stop at number three. If I may offer a practical suggestion born out of experience and years of observation, let me offer the following bit of advice. Once you have decided that you should put into practice some idea that you consider correct and have excluded the opposite as wrong, no longer discuss it with yourself, especially not at the time of execution. This would equivalently annihilate the decision. Instead, do it blindly. I mean it. It is your decision. So why not act on it? Suppose you decide to rise at the first sound of the alarm clock. There's the bed again! Or if you are a religious, the moment you hear the bell for some exercise, never stop to argue the matter. Do not stop to think whether or not you are still busy, or whether it is still early, but immediately move to where you are being called.

If the execution of what you had decided to do costs you some trouble, or if doing it is repugnant to your instincts, in the time between decision and execution do not even think about what you are going to do. Believe me, this is great wisdom. For then all the natural objections will reappear. If you must think about what you are going to do, think only of the good consequences which your undertaking, enlightened by faith, will produce. Some people are such habitual thinkers, they are filled with so many ideas pro and con, on every conceivable aspect of life, that they reduce, if not actually paralyze their potential for literally doing everything for the glory of God.

God surely wants us to know His will. We are also not to jump into action at the first idea that comes to our mind. But I do not think that this is the problem of most people. Most people, I honestly believe, are tempted to postpone what spiritual common sense tells them they should simply do.

The point behind these comments is to help make clear that what God mainly wants of us is this disposition to do His will, this readiness to obey His call, this promptness to listen to His voice. There should be, if I may put it that way, a certain eagerness to do what lies before us as divine Providence is showing. A childlike simplicity such as that of the boy Samuel, who told Yahweh when during the night God called to him: "Speak, Lord, your servant is listening." It was the readiness of Mary when she said to the angel: "Be it done to me according to your word." It was the promptness of Joseph, who upon being told in a dream to take Mary and the Child into Egypt, got up, took the Child and His mother with him and left that night for Egypt.

Prayer of the heart is this kind of prompt, ready, cheerful, immediate doing what God wants of us, though it might be at night, and not waiting for the morning. Or going to Egypt, which means going to a strange land, or entering on some unknown and frightening enterprise. Does this prayer of the heart also include the prayer of suffering? It most certainly does. The complaint is sometimes made that actual prayer is impossible because of illness or a state of great weariness and fatigue. Did not our Lord pray on the cross, and the martyrs on the scaffold? Yes. But for many people actual prayer during sickness or when the body is racked with pain or dead tired is impossible, except perhaps for a moment's whispered "Jesus." Yet who would say that the suffering itself is not a prayer? In fact, the most noble form imaginable. All that is needed is that a person bear his suffering for God, in resignation to His will, with submission and patience in union with the suffering Lord. The heavens, we believe, are pierced by the sound of such prayer. Only the infinite God knows how many graces are conferred on the person suffering and on countless souls besides.

REMAIN IN MY LOVE

Christ had no doubt that His followers could live in the presence of God by practicing this prayer of the heart. That is why the night before He died He told us to "remain in my love," which means abide in my love, stay in it continually. Is there, we might ask, some simple method of keeping oneself, as Christ wants, always in His love? Remember, when we say keeping ourselves in His love, it means excluding self-love. Self is the only competition that God has. Yes, there is a simple method. It has been given various names. But essentially it is practicing contemplation in action by using one's native weaknesses and faults, if you please, to remain in contact with God. Here is how it works. I select some aspiration that expresses the special virtue that I wish to cultivate today, or maybe just this morning, or afternoon or this week or this month. Then I say the aspiration whenever I have a chance to practice the virtue that I think I specially need. When I fail against the virtue, I say the same prayer in reparation for what I've done. I have so many failings and so many tendencies to not live up to this virtue or give in to a given temptation, that all of them become providential occasions for remaining united with God. The value of this method is that by it I multiply acts of virtue with corresponding increase of merits, I make reparation for the faults I commit, and, because such acts of piety are now all indulgenced, I gain additional satisfactory merit from the Church's treasury. All the while I am cultivating the spirit of constant prayer and union with God and supernaturalizing my daily actions.

I want to be as clear as I can in describing what I have been trying to do for years in my own life. It is not just a matter of multiplying aspirations, nor of sacrificing, least of all, mental or vocal prayer, which should also be part of our lives. What's the purpose? The purpose is to integrate our active life with prayer by capitalizing on our weakness and profitting from every manifestation of our lower nature. Depending on one's nature, some people have more of one tendency and less of another. All I have to know is that one person has frequent manifestations of his lower nature. This is what makes sense of St. Paul's, of all things, glorifying in his infirmities! St. Paul? That's me, too! The same with using every temptation of the devil. That is not what the devil intends. But God does. I use every occasion when the devil tempts me to strengthen my love of God. I have a tendency to selfishness. Every time I become aware of it, I say under my breath: "Jesus, my God. I love You above all things." I am oversensitive, and this betrays me into resentment. Whenever that happens, or I feel it is going to happen, I say: "Jesus, make me humble." I may be discouraged because I lack confidence in God. The moment I am aware of what is beginning to happen, I say: "My Jesus, give me courage." I begin to feel smug and self-satisfied, or I have just been praised. That is bad. So I say: "Jesus, make my heart like unto Thine." I am offended or contradicted, and about to lose my patience. So I say, "My Jesus, mercy." I don't mind telling you that on my desk in New York is a 4 x 6 card, folded in half. The face side has the aspiration: "My Jesus, I trust in You."

We still have what I call an epilogue. This conference opened with a question: "How to live in the presence of God?" The answer is too plain to explain. All it takes is to say it. We live in the presence of God by sincerely loving God in everything we do. But no one cheats here. This kind of ceaseless prayer is the disposition of a loving heart, inclining it always to God. It demands no fatiguing attention of the mind, which always remains free to apply itself to whatever God chooses or permits at any moment. My hands, as it were, are free. The secret is to give oneself without selfish attachment. At the first signal, the heart passes with equal detachment to another subject, or another situation. And leave it to God to demand the unexpected! The person who prays thus, prays almost without thinking. No one but God knows what he or she is really doing. No one suffers, or is inconvenienced. The work is done. In fact, you could say that whatever that person is doing, or wherever he or she is going, they carry this prayer along with them. It is never interrupted, except perhaps in sleep. But even then, one may truly say like the spouse in the Canticles: "I sleep, but my heart is awake." That is the kind of a heart we are talking about.

All that it takes, but it belongs to its essence, is that we love God with our whole heart, and we prove that we do by always trying to please Him. The beauty of thus living in the presence of God is that He returns the favor by living, as it were, in the presence of us. A strange expression to use of God, but it is a familiar experience to those who understand.

Daughters of St. Paul

MASSACHUSETTS
 50 St. Paul's Ave., Jamaica Plain, Boston, MA 02130; **617-522-8911.**
 172 Tremont Street, Boston, MA 02111; **617-426-5464; 617-426-4230.**
NEW YORK
 78 Fort Place, Staten Island, NY 10301; **212-447-5071; 212-447-5086.**
 59 East 43rd Street, New York, NY 10017; **212-986-7580.**
 625 East 187th Street, Bronx, NY 10458; **212-584-0440.**
 525 Main Street, Buffalo, NY 14203; **716-847-6044.**
NEW JERSEY
 Hudson Mall—Route 440 and Communipaw Ave.,
  Jersey City, NJ 07304; **201-433-7740.**
CONNECTICUT
 202 Fairfield Ave., Bridgeport, CT 06604; **203-335-9913.**
OHIO
 2105 Ontario Street (at Prospect Ave.), Cleveland, OH 44115; **216-621-9427.**
 616 Walnut Street, Cincinnati, OH 45202; **513-421-5733; 513-721-5059.**
PENNSYLVANIA
 1719 Chestnut Street, Philadelphia, PA 19103; **215-568-2638; 215-864-0991.**
VIRGINIA
 1025 King Street, Alexandria, VA 22314; **703-683-1741; 703-549-3806.**
SOUTH CAROLINA
 243 King Street, Charleston, SC 29401.
FLORIDA
 2700 Biscayne Blvd., Miami, FL 33137; **305-573-1618; 305-573-1624.**
LOUISIANA
 4403 Veterans Memorial Blvd., Metairie, LA 70006; **504-887-7631;**
  504-887-0113.
 423 Main Street, Baton Rouge, LA 70802; **504-343-4057; 504-381-9485.**
MISSOURI
 1001 Pine Street (at North 10th), St. Louis, MO 63101; **314-621-0346;**
  314-231-1034.
ILLINOIS
 172 North Michigan Ave., Chicago, IL 60601; **312-346-4228; 312-346-3240.**
TEXAS
 114 Main Plaza, San Antonio, TX 78205; **512-224-8101; 512-224-0938.**
CALIFORNIA
 1570 Fifth Ave., San Diego, CA 92101; **619-232-1442.**
 46 Geary Street, San Francisco, CA 94108; **415-781-5180.**
WASHINGTON
 2301 Second Ave., Seattle, WA 98121 **206-623-1320; 206-623-2234.**
HAWAII
 1143 Bishop Street, Honolulu, HI 96813; **808-521-2731.**
ALASKA
 750 West 5th Ave., Anchorage, AK 99501; **907-272-8183.**